Three CENTURIES of INFECTIOUS DISEASE

AN ILLUSTRATED HISTORY OF RESEARCH AND TREATMENT

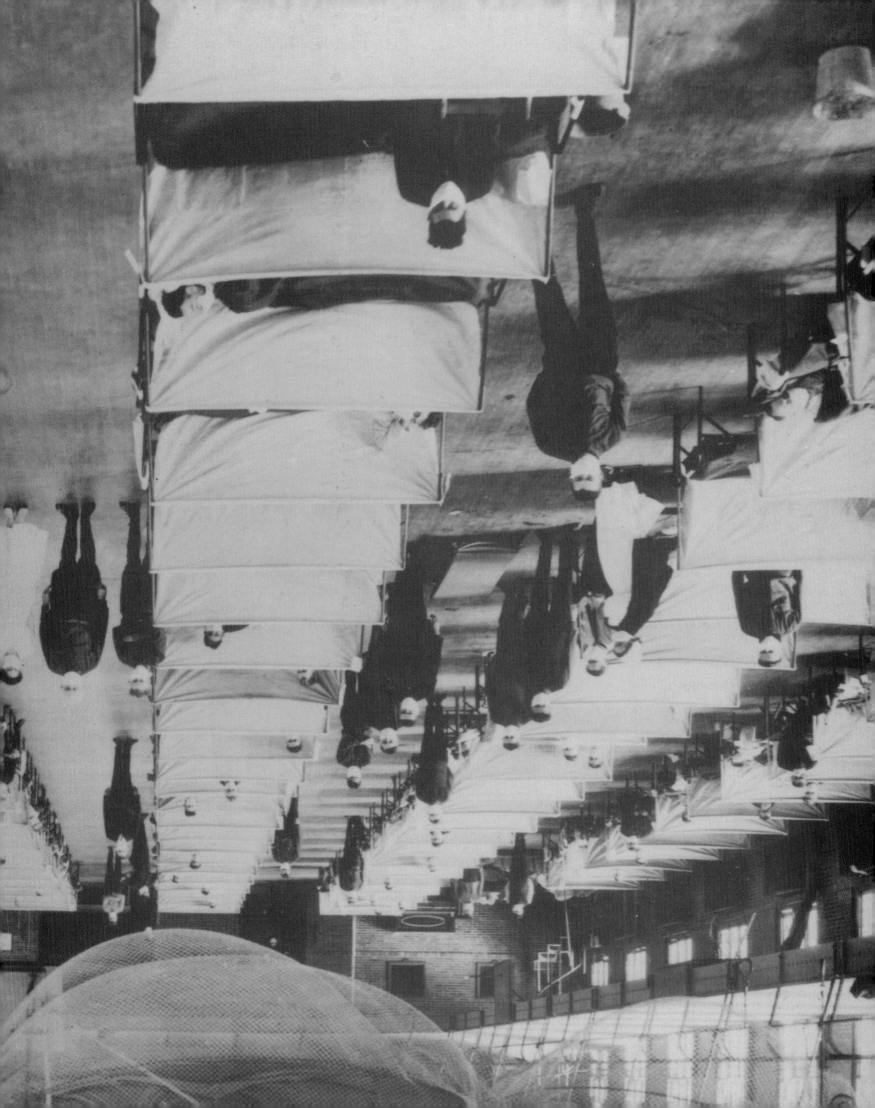

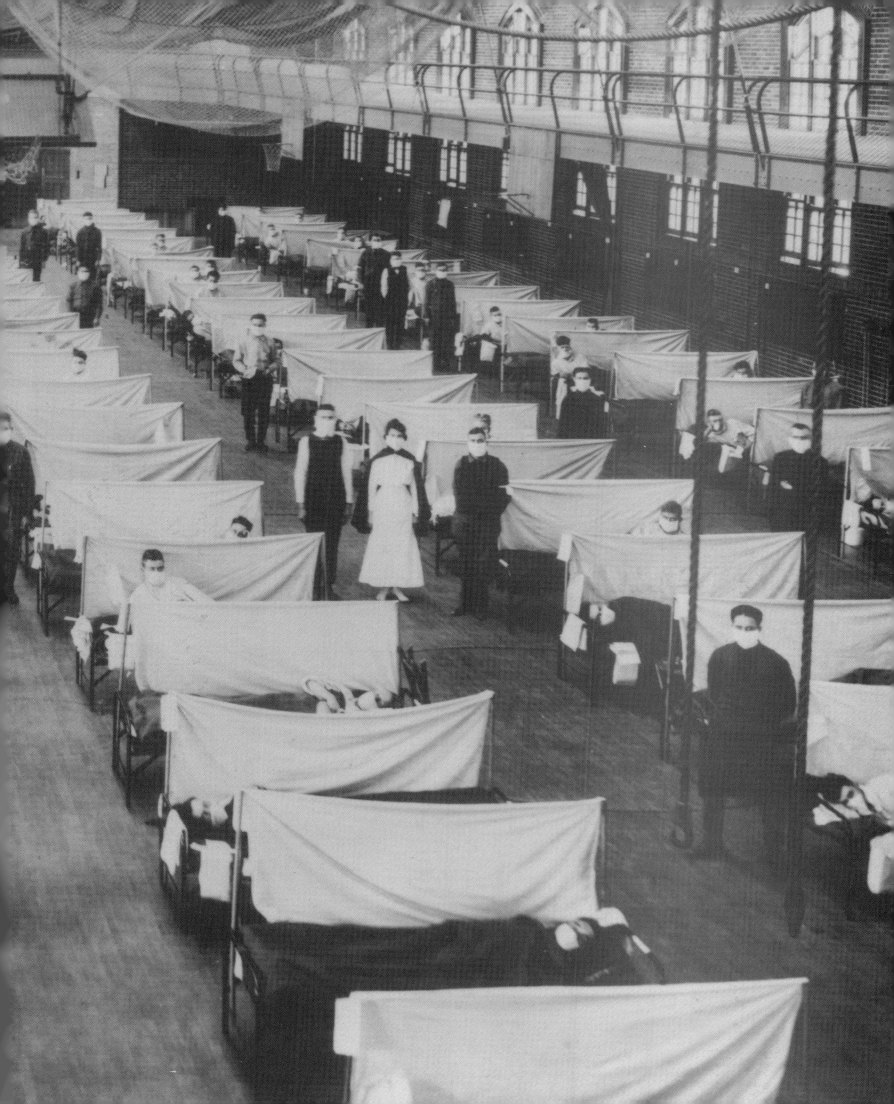

Three
CENTURIES of
INFECTIOUS DISEASE

AN ILLUSTRATED HISTORY OF RESEARCH AND TREATMENT

with commentary by

WENDY B. MURPHY

GP Greenwich Press
Greenwich, Connecticut

Copyright ©1998 Greenwich Press

Greenwich Press
500 West Putnam Avenue
Greenwich, CT 06830

ISBN: 1-57013-066-3

Publisher: Corey Kupersmith, RPh
Editorial Director: Lois Gandt
Copy Editor: Patrice Hibbard
Art Director: Jill Ruscoll
Designer: Megan Youngquist

Cover photo: Library of Congress

Every effort has been made to ensure the medical and historical accuracy of this book. The author regrets any errors, either of fact or omission.

Printed in USA

Contents

Introduction

Controlling infectious diseases is practicing the art of the possible. The graphic images in this book attest to some of the great triumphs in our relentless struggle against the invisible microbes that beset humankind in our work and our homes, in our leisure activities, and even in our lovemaking. During this generation we have witnessed the eradication of smallpox, one of the greatest scourges of recorded history, whose virulent eruptions have caused severe disfigurement, blindness, and death. Bubonic plague has virtually disappeared from the medical landscape.

During this generation we have witnessed the eradication of smallpox, one of the greatest scourges of recorded history, whose virulent eruptions have caused severe disfigurement, blindness, and death. Bubonic plague has virtually disappeared from the medical landscape.

Progress in vaccines has had a major impact on transmission of many diseases. Tetanus, diphtheria, and pertussis, the classic ingredients of the triple vaccine, have been remarkably reduced where the vaccine is utilized. Since the polio vaccines were developed in the 1950s, this disease has come under control in the developed countries; in recent years, the WHO campaign has produced eradication of polio in the Americas and is making inroads in controlling polio in Africa and Asia, where the disease is still active. The measles vaccine is highly effective, curbing the disease in most developed countries, but it is still epidemic and dangerous in many developing countries. For many of the classic infectious diseases for which vaccines are available, the challenge is no longer scientific but has shifted to the economic front.

Several diseases have come under control, only to recrudesce in recent times, often reflecting socioeconomic conditions in the endemic area. Thus, malaria control was highly successful but has fallen victim to its earlier success with recent and persistent disease in the same regions, now devoid of experienced personnel and resources. This new wave of malaria cases is propelled by resistance to antimalarial drugs in parasites and diminished effectiveness of insecticides in mosquitoes.

In most areas of the world, improvements in sanitation and health facilities have led to fewer childhood deaths and extended life expectancy. Antibiotics have prevented early fatalities due to infections of the respiratory tract. Oral rehydration has saved many lives in children with dehydrating diarrhea. The toll of infectious diseases is improving in most countries. As infections decline, an increase in cardiovascular disease and cancer is occurring, but mostly in older persons who have survived earlier assaults of infection.

Yet, the microbes are not remaining in a vanquished state. Microorganisms have proven again and again that they are better biochemists than their hosts, and they have spawned new waves of antibiotic-resistant progeny. The pneumococcus has acquired resistance to its initial adversary, penicillin, causing great concern as these strains spread across the globe. Many of the gram-negative bacilli that cause typhoid fever, urinary tract infection, and gastroenteritis have developed substantial resistance to conventional antibiotics. Unless we learn to rein in our use of antibiotics, we stand in danger of losing them as partners in fighting these pathogens.

Any discussion of infection would be remiss without mentioning the most important pestilence of our age, human immunodeficiency virus. This contagion seems to have arisen spontaneously in central Africa, without antecedents in prior use of drugs or chemicals or any historical event that could presage its emergence. The virus strikes rich and poor, young and old, male and female, with no heed to national borders, religious preferences, or family units. Its spread has, thus far, defied public health interventions, except in a few important areas where education in safe sex practices is making a difference. Most experts agree that a vaccine would be the most efficacious approach to control.

Despite these new adversities and emerging infections, the human spirit has a seemingly endless capacity to confront and overcome them. The pictures in this book recall past plagues and pestilences over which we have triumphed. As we confront new challenges, we can gain comfort and strength from these reminders of our past accomplishments.

SHERWOOD L. GORBACH, MD

Professor of Family Medicine, Community Health and Microbiology and Immunology
Tufts University School of Medicine

Attending Physician
New England Medical Center and St. Elizabeth's Hospital
Boston, Massachusetts

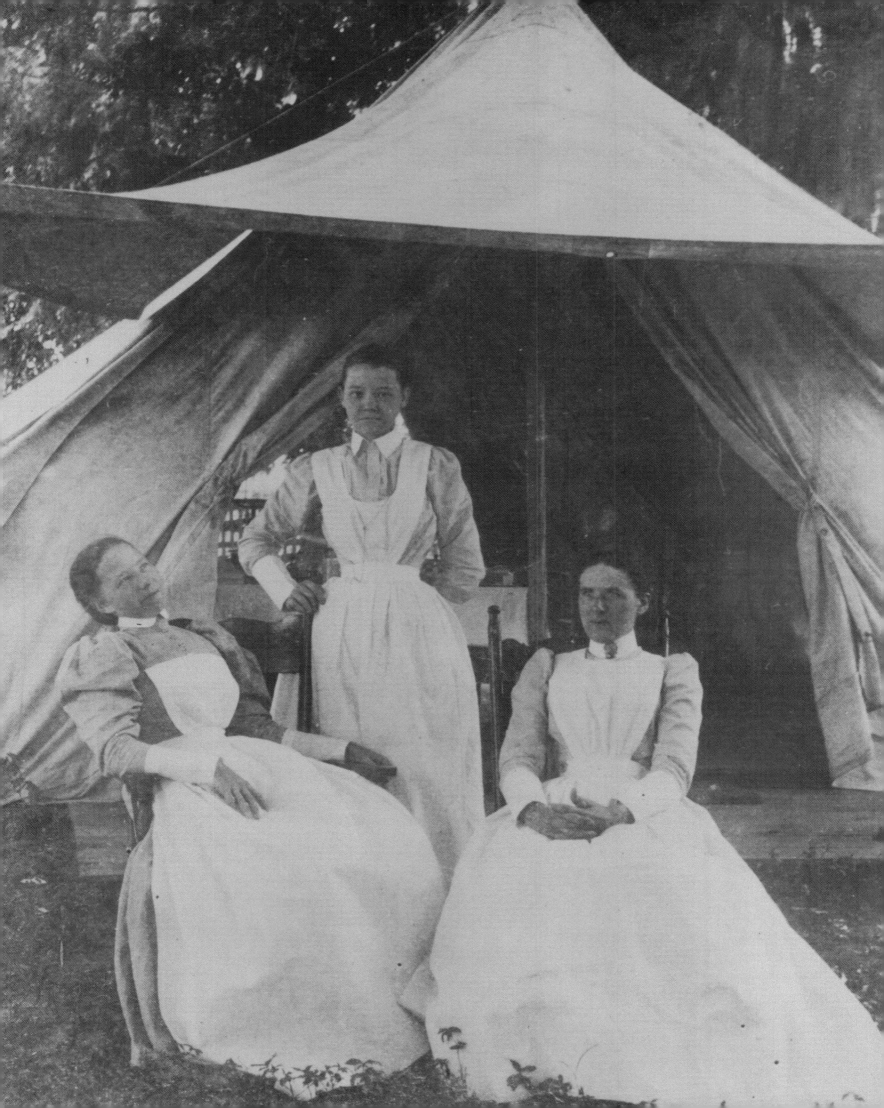

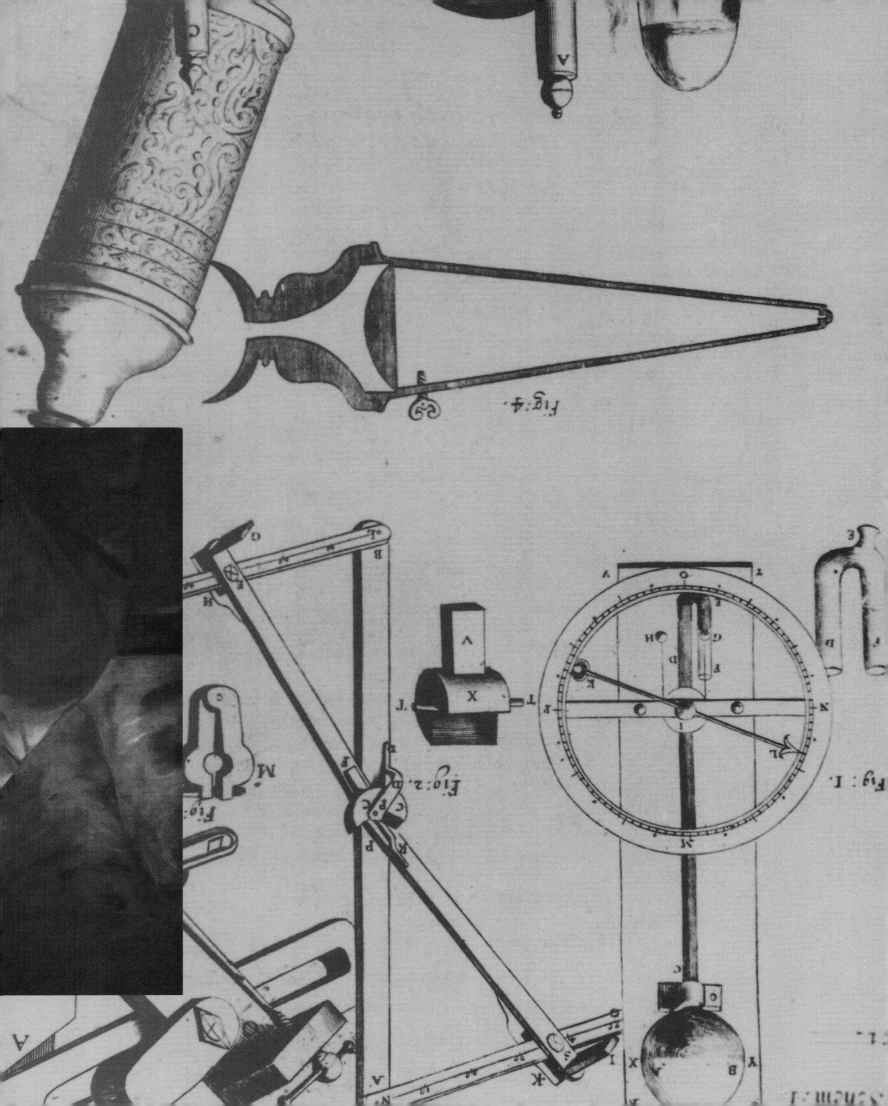

Chapter 1

*If the **humors** were in balance, a person felt **well**; if they were out of harmony, **sickness** was the **certain result**.*

The Age of Humors

The   Beginning   to   1799

Until very recently, the cause or causes of **infectious disease** was a subject of anxious debate in the Western world. Underlying virtually all explanations lay the doctrine of humoral pathology. As described by the Greek physician Hippocrates, man's health and temperament were affected by four bodily fluids or "humors"—blood, phlegm, black bile, and yellow bile. If the humors were in balance, a person felt well; if they were out of harmony, sickness was the certain result. Seeking a force capable of causing such deadly disease, the medieval sages fastened on the heavenly bodies as agents, and they developed the "science" of astrology to track celestial influences.

According to this system of beliefs, persons—and even whole societies—succumbed to plagues and pestilences when the stars were misaligned. Comets in particular were taken as harbingers of coming pests and plagues. Only by restoring the balance of humors with heroic remedies could anyone hope to regain equilibrium. Healers consequently subjected their patients to bloodletting, sweating, emetics, laxatives, enemas, and a battery of magical potions until the unfortunates either died of exhaustion or somehow triumphed over their treatment.

While humoralism continued to be the fundamental explanation of all things medical in the 17th and 18th centuries, cracks in the foundation began to appear. Some scientifically minded Europeans developed a number of tools and techniques that revealed more earthly, mechanistic explanations for certain diseases and their symptoms. Among the trailblazers for this new view were the English physicians William Harvey and Thomas Sydenham.

Harvey published the first accurate description of the human circulatory system in 1628; Sydenham's *Observationes Medicae*, 1676, presented the first detailed clinical observations of what he rightly regarded as a collection of distinctly different human diseases requiring different medical treatments; it was widely believed at the time that all diseases were symptomatic variations on a single condition, inflammation. Two other pioneers, naturalists Anton van Leeuwenhoek and Robert Hooke, were among the earliest to grasp the value of the microscope in examining the minutiae of disease, opening the way to the eventual discovery and physical description of bacteria.

Ironically, such instances of enlightenment came at a time when the behavior of contagions was changing. Whereas diseases had typically been expressed in a variety of endemic scourges chiefly affecting small children and the infirm elderly at a predictable but slow rate (chicken pox, influenza, measles, mumps, scarlet fever, smallpox, and tuberculosis were the most common killers), many of these same diseases as well as a host of new ones were erupting without warning; sometimes they swept like juggernauts through nations and even whole continents before subsiding. Suddenly, no one seemed safe.

In the 17th century, scarcely a city in Europe escaped at least one encounter with bubonic plague. The Venetian Republic lost over 500 000 to plague in 1630 and London's Great Plague of 1665 carried away an estimated 100 000. We now know that the changes in the patterns of infection sweeping Europe and the world beginning in the 15th century were due to a combination of factors. Increasing urbanization created more and larger breeding grounds for disease in Europe. Added to this was the expansion of commerce and the growing movement of masses of peoples, which exposed them to infectious agents hitherto unknown. But from the perspective of Europeans steeped in myth and misinformation, the evidence of their new vulnerability was as inexplicable as it was terrifying.

Two other pioneers, naturalists Anton van Leeuwenhoek and Robert Hooke, were among the earliest to grasp the value of the microscope in examining the minutiae of disease, opening the way to the eventual discovery and physical description of bacteria.

With African contact, for example, yellow fever, malaria, and a host of parasitic diseases were unleashed in Europe; European explorers and traders, for their part, injected smallpox and tuberculosis into Africa's vulnerable populations. In the New World, European contact was, if possible, even more calamitous to the indigenous peoples. Indeed, the variety of scourges (13 by one count) imported not only from Europe but also from Africa with the Colonial slave trade effectively annihilated many native populations in the Caribbean and, later on, mainland America. As to infectious diseases that the New World gave the Old, the only significant disease that may eventually be shown to have origins in this hemisphere is syphilis, although it seems equally plausible that European sailors brought this venereal disease with them.

Whatever the truth of syphilis' origins, most early European settlements in North America enjoyed a slightly lower rate of mortality from infectious diseases than their counterparts in Europe. This was chiefly because their communities were thinly populated and contact with outsiders—the source of most contagions—was relatively infrequent. Sanitary laws concerning safe food, drinking water, and waste removal, while they existed "on the books" in most places, were only partially observed; but again, the fact of small-town life worked to spare most people from the worst effects of poor public and personal housekeeping. And to limit the two most feared diseases in Colonial America—smallpox and yellow fever—every port town had its quarantine laws by which the sick were either kept away entirely or put into isolation in the local "pest house." Nonetheless, when disease did penetrate a community, its effects were likely to be devastating to all ages. Diphtheria, which seems to have arrived with the early Puritans of Massachusetts Bay Colony, was a regular visitor in many communities by the 18th century. Children were the principal victims. In 1735, when an epidemic ran through parts of New England, reportedly killing 1000 individuals, 900 of them were youngsters. That year in one small New Hampshire village alone, 20 families lost all their children to diphtheria within a matter of days. Given the intensely spiritual flavor of the time, such events were often understood in religious and moral terms, with an epidemic seen as a form of godly retribution for sins of the community.

Disease treatments in the Colonies were equally misguided. They ranged from helpless waiting to the heroic measures typically practiced by physicians in urban centers. Philadelphia's Benjamin Rush was convinced that "there is but one disease in the world" and its underlying cause was "convulsive excitement" within the walls of blood vessels. To relieve this mortifying tension, he prescribed purging patients with "ten-and-ten," a violent cathartic consisting of ten grains of calomel and ten grains of jalap, combined with copious bloodletting. Popular as a hero of the American Revolution, and a leader in medical education, Rush's views unfortunately prevailed over those of more moderate physicians until well into the 19th century.

EVER SINCE THE ARRIVAL OF BUBONIC PLAGUE in England in the 14th century, London had regularly succumbed to epidemics that caused tremendous social disruptions. In this woodcut of the Plague Year of 1665, Londoners are seen fleeing the teeming city in droves. In a futile effort to control the spread of disease, government officials imposed a "quarantine," so called because it lasted 40 days, on plague houses with red crosses and notices reading "Lord, have mercy." Carts were deployed to carry away the dead, and dogcatchers assigned to slaughter dogs, erroneously believed to be transmitters of plague. By summer, a horrid stench filled the air, and whole neighborhoods stood abandoned. Only with the return of cold weather did the number of new cases wane, leaving a final official tally of 68 596 dead, though modern estimates are much higher.

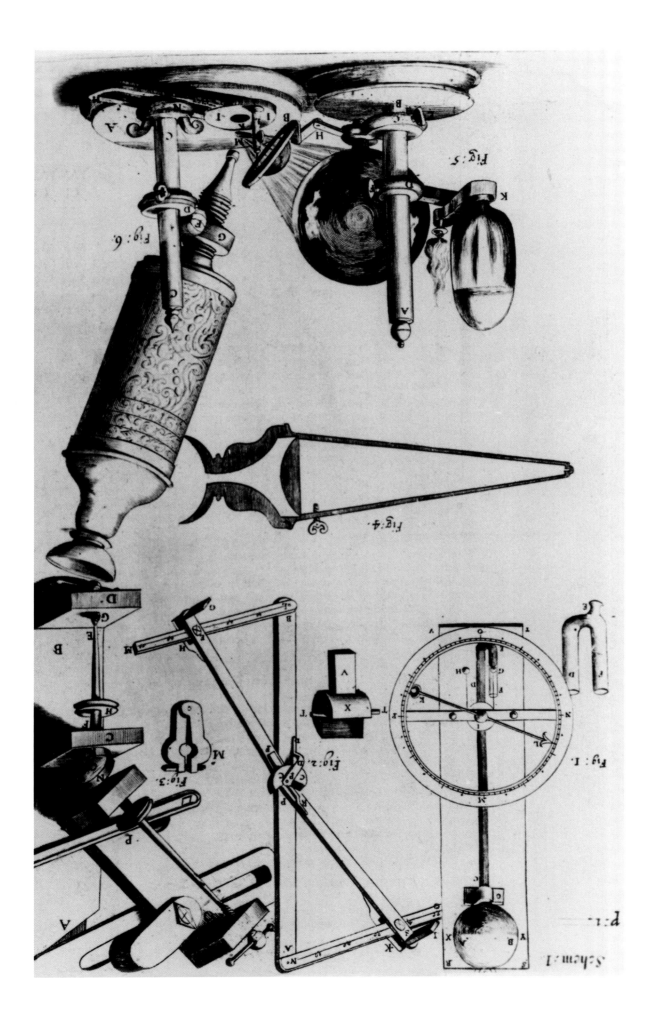

A CRITICAL EARLY STEP TOWARD UNDERSTANDING the causes of infectious diseases lay in devising the means to see the organisms of contagion. The magnifying glass had been known since at least the 13th century, but it was not until the 17th century that a practical tool was developed. The Dutchman Anton van Leeuwenhoek is generally credited with devising the first simple microscope. High magnification was possible only with the development of a compound microscope, containing at least two lenses. This improvement was achieved in 1662 by the Englishman Robert Hooke. The illustration (left) from his *Micrographia*, published in 1665, shows his remarkable microscope, a lens grinding machine, and various other inventions. Right, physicians attempting to avoid contagion sometimes took extreme measures. This engraving shows the robe and helmet worn by doctors in plague-ridden Germany in 1656. The beak is filled with spices, supposedly to filter the evil air.

IN THE WAKE OF EUROPEAN EXPLORATION, Old World diseases, especially smallpox, influenza, and measles, devastated the peoples of the New World. These once remarkably healthy people traditionally lived in small, isolated groups in environments that were virtually without human contaminants. Diseases stemming from contact with domesticated animals were also unknown to Native Americans before Columbus' time, because farming and herding were not practiced. This 17th century European engraving shows a group of Native Americans preparing to bury their dead.

A BRIEF RULE

To guide the Common-People of
NEW-ENGLAND
How to order themselves and theirs in the
Small Pocks, or Meafels.

The *small Pox* (whofe nature and cure the *Meafels* follow) is a difeafe in the blood, endeavouring to recover a new form and ftate.

2. This nature attempts---1. By Separation of the impure from the pure, thrufting it out from the Veins to the Flefh.---2. By driving out the impure from the Flefh to the Skin.

3. The firft Separation is done in the firft four dayes by a Feaverifh boyling (Ebullition) of the Blood, laying down the impurities in the Flefhy parts which kindly effected the Feaverifh tumult is calmed.

4. The fecond Separation from the Flefh to the Skin, or *Superficies* is done through the reft of the time of the difeafe.

5 There are feveral Errors in ordering thefe fick ones in both thefe Operations of Nature which prove very dangerous and commonly deadly either by overmuch haftening Nature beyond its own pace, or in hindering of it from its own vigorous operation.

6 The Separation by Ebullition in the Feaverifh heat is over heightned by too much Clothes, too hot a room, hot *Cordials*, as *Diafcordium, Gafcons powder* and fuch like, for hence come *Phrenzies*, dangerous exceffive fweats, or the flowing of the Pocks into one overfpreading fore, vulgarly called the Flox.

7. The fame feperation is overmuch hindred by prepofterous cooling that Feaverifh boyling heat, by *Bloodletting, Glifters, Vomits, purges*, or *cooling medicines*. For though thefe many times haften the coming forth of the *Pox*, yet they take away that fupply which fhould keep them out till they are ripe, wherefore they fink in again to the deadly danger of the fick.

8. If a *Phrenfie* happen, or through a *Plethorie* (that is fulnefs of blood) the Circulation of the blood be hindred, and thereupon the whole mafs of blood choaked up, then either let blood, Or fee that their diet, or medicines be not altogether cooling, but let them in no wife be hearing, therefore let him lye no otherwife covered in his bed then he was wont in health: His Chamber not made hot with fire if the weather be temperate, let him drink fmall Beer only warm'd with a Toft, let him fup up thin *water-gruel*, or *water pottage* made only of Indian Flour and water, inftead of *Oat-meal*: Let him eat *boild App'es*: But I would not advife at this time any medicine befides. By this means that exceffive Ebullition (or boyling of his blood) will by degrees abate, and the Symptoms ceafe; If not, but the blood be fo inraged that it will admit no delay, then either let blood (if Age will bear it) or elfe give fome notably cooling medicine, or refrefh him with more free Air.

9. But if the boiling of the blood be weak and dull that there is caufe to fear it is not able to work a Separation, as it's wont to be in fuch as have been let blood, or are fat, or Flegmatick, or brought low by fome other ficknefs or labour of the (*Gonorrhea*) running of the Reins, or fome other Evacuation: In fuch Cafes, *Cordials* muft drive them out, or they muft dy.

10. In time of driving out the *Pocks* from the Flefh, here care muft be had that the *Puftules* keep out in a right meafure till they have attain'd their end without going in again, for that is deadly.

11. In this time take heed when the *Puftules* appear whilft not yet ripe, leaft by too much heat there arife a new *Ebullition* (or Feaverifh boyling) for this troubles the driving out , or brings back the feparated parts into the blood , or the Flefhy parts overheated are difabled from a right fuppuration or laftly the temper of the blood and tone of the Flefh is fo perverted that it cannot overcome and digeft the matter driven out.

12. Yet on the other hand the breaking out muft not be hindred, by expofing the fick unto the cold. The degree of heat muft be fuch as is natural agrees with the temper of the flefhy parts: That waich exceeds or falls fhort is dangerous: Therefore the feafon of the year, Age of the fick, and their manner of life here require a difcreet and different Confideration, requiring the Counfel of an expert Phyfitian.

13. But if by any error a new *Ebullition* arifeth, the fame art muft be ufed to allay it as is before expreft.

14. If the *Puftules* go in and a flux of the belly follows (for elfe there is no fuch danger) then *Cordials* are to be ufed, yet moderate and not too often for fear of new *Ebullition*.

15. If much fpitting (*Ptyalifmus*) follow, you may hope all will go well, therefore by no means hinder it : Only with warm fmall Beer let their mouths be wafhed.

16. When the *Puftules* are dryed and fallen, purge well, efpecially if it be in Autumn.

17. As foon as this difeafe therefore appears by its figns, let the fick abftein from Flefh and Wine, and open Air, let him ufe fmall Bear warmed with a Toft for his ordinary drink, and moderately when he defires it. For food ufe *water-gruel, water-pottage*, and other things having no manifeft hot quality, eafy of digeftion, boild Apples, and milk fometimes for change, but the coldnefs taken off. Let the ufe of his bed be according to the feafon of the year, and the multitude of the *Pocks*, or as found perfons

are wont: In Summer let him rife according to cuftome, yet fo as to be defended both from heat and cold in Excefs, the difeafe will be the fooner over and lefs troublefome, for being kept in bed nourifheth the Feaverifh heat and makes the *Pocks* break out with a painful inflamation.

19. In a colder feafon, and breaking forth of a multitude of *Puftules*, forcing the fick to keep his bed, let him be covered according to his cuftome in health, a moderate fire in the winter being kindled in his Chamber, morning and Evening: neither need he keep his Arms alwayes in bed, or ly ftill in the fame place, for fear leaft he fhould fweat which is very dangerous efpecially to youth.

20. Before the fourth day ufe no medicines to drive out, nor be too ftrict with the fick; for by how much the more gently the *Puftules* do grow, by fo much the fuller and perfecter will the Separation be.

21. On the fourth day a gentle *Cordial* may help once given.

22. From that time a fmall draught of warm milk (not hot) a little dy'd with *Saffron* may be given morning and evening till the *Puftules* are come to their due greatnefs and ripenefs.

23. When the *Puftules* begin to dry and cruft, leaft the rotten vapours ftrike inward, which fometimes caufeth fudden death; Take morning and evening fome temperate *Cordial* as four or five fpoonfuls of *Malaga wine* tinged with a little *Saffron*.

24. When the *Puftules* are dryd and fallen off, purge once and again, efpecially in the *Autumn Pocks*.

25. Beware of anointing with *Oils, Fatts, Ointments*, and fuch defenfives, for keeping the corrupted matter in the *Puftules* from drying up, by tho moifture they fret deeper into the Flefh, and fo make the more deep Scarrs.

26. The young and lively men that are brought to a plentiful fweat in this ficknefs, about the eighth day the fweat ftops of it felf, by no means afterwards to be drawn out again; the fick thereupon feels moft troublefome difreft and anguifh, and then makes abundance of water and fo dyes.

Few young men and ftrong thus handled efcape, except they fall into abundance of fpitting or plentiful bleeding at the nofe.

27. Signs difcovering the Affault at firft are beating pain in the head, Forehead and temples, pain in the back, great fleepinefs, gliftring of the eyes, (fhining glimmerings feem before them, itching of them alfo, with tears flowing of themfelves, itching of the Nofe, fhort breath, dry Cough, oft neezing, hoarfenefs, heat, rednefs, and fenfe of pricking over the whole body, terrors in the fleep, forrow and reftlefsnefs, beating of the hearts, *Urine* fometimes as in health, fometime filthy from great *Ebullition*, and all this or many of thefe with a Feaverifh diftemper.

28. Signs warning of the probable Event. If they break forth eafily, quickly, and foon come to ripening, if the Symptomes be gentle, the Feaver mild, and after the breaking forth it abat S If the voice be free, and breathing eafie, efpecially if the Pox be red white diftinct, foft few, round, fharp top'd, only without and not in the inward parts; if there be large bleeding at the nofe. Thefe figns are hopeful.

29. But fuch figns are doubtful, when they difficultly appear, when they fink in again, when they are black, blewifh, green, hard, all in one, if the Feaver abate not with their breaking forth, if there be Swooning, difficulty of breathing, great thirft, quinfey, great unquietnefs, and it is very dangerous, if there be ioyn'd with it fome other malignant Feaver, called by fome the peftilential Pox: the *Spotted Feaver* is oft joyned with it.

30 Deadly Signs if the *Flux* of the *Belly* happen, when they are broke forth, if the Urine be bloody, or black, or the *Ordure* of that Colour; Or if pure blood be caft out by the Belly or Gumms: Thefe Signs are for the moft part deadly.

Thefe things have I written Candid Reader, *not to imform the Learned* Phyfician *that hath much more caufe to underftand what pertains to this difeafe than I, but to give fome light to thofe that have not fuch advantages, leaving the difficulty of this difeafe to the* Phyfitians *Art, wifdome, and Faithfulnefs: for the right managing of them in the whole Courfe of the difeafe tends both to the Patients fafety, and the* Phyfitians *defired Succefs in his Adminiftration: For in vain is the* Phyfitians *Art imployed, if they are not under a Regular Regiment. I am, though no* Phyfitian, *yet a well wifher to the fick: And therefore intreating the Lord to turn our hearts, and ftay his hand, I am*

A Friend, Reader to thy
Welfare,

Thomas Thacher.

21. 11, 167⅞.

BOSTON, Printed and fold by *John Fofter*. 1677.

SMALLPOX WAS AN EARLY SCOURGE OF EUROPEAN COLONISTS IN NORTH AMERICA, with periodic epidemics almost as much a threat to them as to native populations. This broadside, published in 1677, was written "not to inform the Learned Physician ... but to give some light to those that have not such advantages," whom the author described as "the Common People." It was written by Dr. Thomas Thacher, a physician and minister who settled in New England in 1635. The paper is generally regarded as the first medical treatise printed in North America.

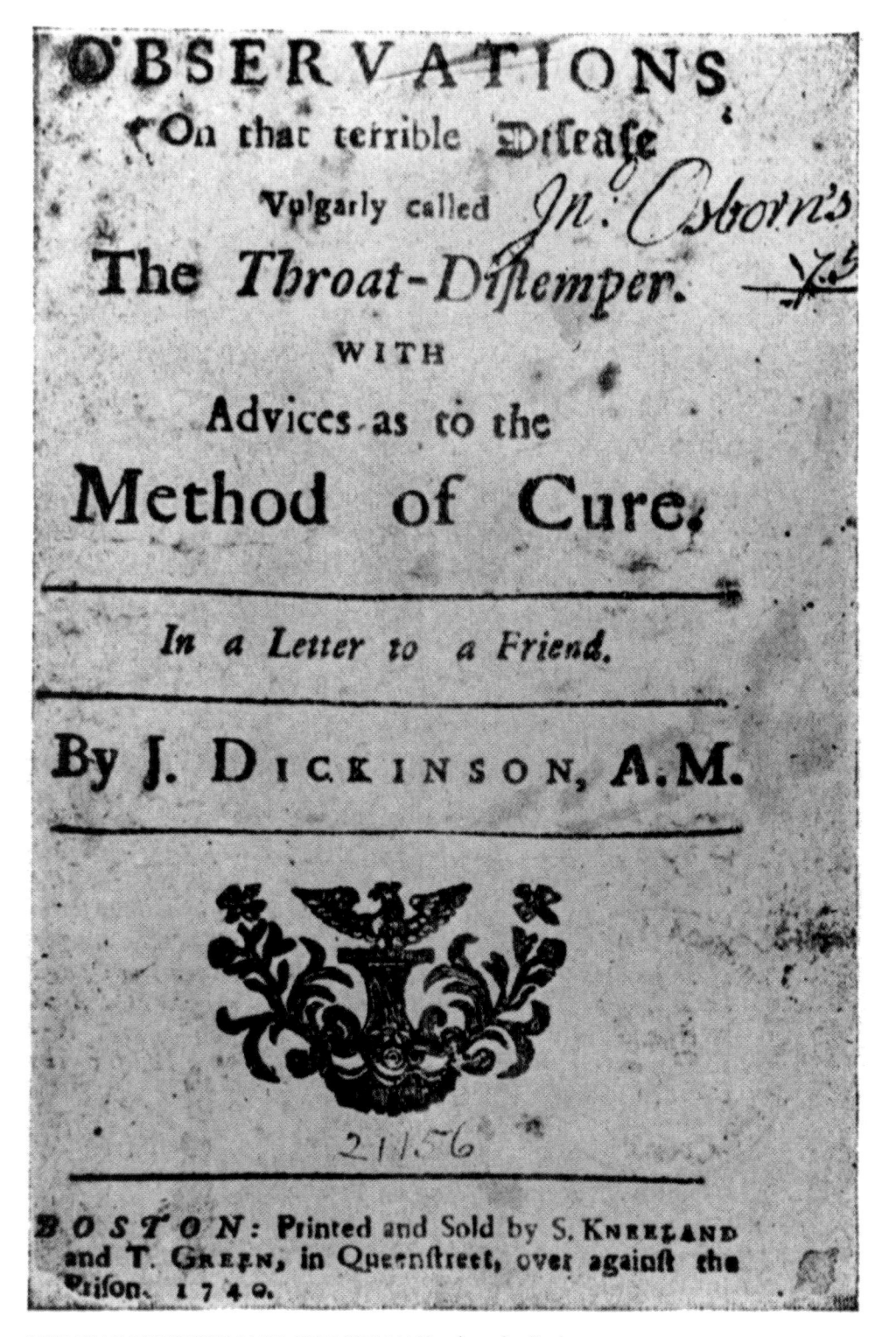

OBSERVATIONS,
On that terrible Diseafe
Vulgarly called *Jn. Osborn's*
The *Throat-Diftemper*.

WITH

Advices as to the

Method of Cure,

In a Letter to a Friend.

By J. DICKINSON, A.M.

21156

BOSTON: Printed and Sold by S. KNEELAND
and T. GREEN, in Queenftreet, over againft the
Prifon. 1740.

DIPHTHERIA WAS RECORDED IN THE COLONIES IN 1659, when the Puritan preacher Increase Mather reported a "Malady of Bladders in the Windpipe" among children in the Massachusetts Bay Colony. Emergency tracheotomies to aid breathing were the singular remedy for this bacterial disease, which sometimes also included a virulent phage virus as well. A more detailed report of the disease appeared in J. Dickinson's *Throat-Distemper*, which was published following a severe epidemic that erupted in New England in 1735 and spread gradually into the mid-Atlantic Colonies. Dickinson noted that its first appearance in his community had been in a family who lost eight children in a fortnight.

TRAINED IN SCOTLAND AND LONDON,
Benjamin Rush of Philadelphia became
the most influential 18th-century physician
in America, and his teachings extended well
beyond his own life span. A signer of the
Declaration of Independence, Rush taught
chemistry and medicine at the University
of Pennsylvania. In 1786 he founded the
Philadelphia Dispensary, the first outpatient
clinic for the poor in the nation. As befitted
his time, Rush practiced "heroic medicine,"
much of it based upon the tenets of the
English theorist John Brown, who classified
all diseases as either "sthenic" (caused by
an excess of stimulation) or "asthenic" (an
insufficiency of stimulation). Like Brown,
Rush also rejected strongly any notions
that diseases might have multiple causes
or agents.

RUSH BELIEVED IN MASSIVE PURGING and blood-letting—up to six to eight pints of blood over two days—as the best medicine for all sorts of diseases. Some of the instruments Rush might use to bleed his patients were lancets and scarifiers. Another method of bloodletting involved leeches. Physicians could stock up on a fresh supply of the blood-sucking worms at their local pharmacy, where ornamental leech jars like this one were always prominently displayed.

LIKE ALL DOCTORS OF THE PERIOD, Benjamin Rush kept a well-stocked chest of medicaments and tools. Rush's medicine chest (right) includes lancets, cupping glasses, a hand-held apothecary scale and weights, a glass mortar and pestle, and a spatula for compounding pills. The back of the chest displays a collection of herbals and chemicals in bottles and boxes. For influenza, Rush might mix up arsenicum and mercurius; for scarlet fever, aconite and belladonna; for mumps, belladonna followed by mercurius; and for "hooping cough," a regimen including belladonna, ipecac, pulsatilla, and sulphur.

RUSH WAS PARTICULARLY CELEBRATED for his steadfast care of patients during the 1793 epidemic of yellow fever that killed 4000 in Philadelphia alone. The disease had become endemic on mainland North America, having arrived several decades earlier with the beginnings of the African slave trade. But the outbreak in August 1793 was notably more violent than any in memory. News of the disease's spread quickly reached surrounding towns like Burlington, New Jersey, where broadsides like this one were posted to alert citizens. The fever raged until late October, when mysteriously it came to a sudden and dramatic end.

AT a MEETING of the Corporation of the city of Burlington, August 30th, 1793, the following recommendations to the citizens was unanimously agreed to.

WHEREAS there is great reason for caution against the malignant Fever or contagious disorder, which prevails in Philadelphia, and it is our duty to use every probable means to prevent the same in the city of Burlington; the Corporation of Burlington after collecting every advice which could be obtained,

RECOMMEND to the Citizens of Burlington,

1. That all unnecessary intercourse be avoided with Philadelphia, that no dry goods, woollen cloths, woollens, cottons or linens, or any packages where straw, hay or shavings are used, be imported within twenty days.

2. That the masters of the boats which ply to and from Burlington to Philadelphia, be very careful that they do not receive on board their vessels, or bring to this city within twenty days, any person or persons but those who appear in good health.

3. That no animal or vegetable substances be thrown or permitted to lay in the streets or alleys, but that all offals, water-melon rinds and substances that putrefy be thrown into the delaware or buried.

4. That no water be permitted to stagnate about the pumps, in the streets or near any houses; but that the wharves, streets, alleys and gutters, ditches, house, and barnyards, be kept as clean as possible.

5. The Physicians in Burlington are requested to make report to the Mayor or Recorder as soon as possible, after they shall have been called to and visited any person or persons, who shall have the said malignant Fever.

Signed by order of the Corporation,

BOWES REED, *Mayor.*

The following means to prevent the contagion is recommended by the College of Physicians in Philadelphia.

" To avoid all fatigue of body and mind."

" To avoid standing or sitting in the sun, also in a current of air, or in the evening air."

" To accommodate the dress to the weather, and to exceed rather in warm than in cool cloathing."

" To avoid intemperance, but to use fermented liquors, such as wine, beer and cyder with moderation."

" The burning of gunpowder, the use of vinegar and camphor upon handkerchiefs or in smelling bottles, particularly by persons whose duty calls them to visit or attend the sick."

Published by order of the Corporation,

ABRAHAM GARDINER, *Clerk.*

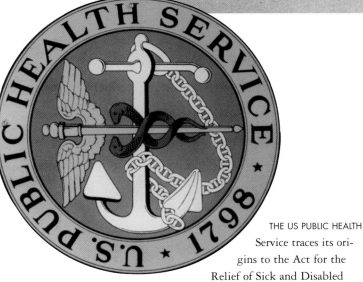

Custom House, Boston

78

Sir—The bearer _____ *is entitled to the priviliges of the* **MARINE HOSPITAL.**

Your Obedt. Servt.

The Physician of the Marine Hospital Chelsea _____ *Collector.*

THE FIRST MARINE HOSPITAL constructed was the 1802 facility in Charlestown, located on the eastern flank of Boston harbor. Many others followed, in Newport, Rhode Island; on New York's Staten Island; in Charleston, South Carolina; Norfolk, Virginia; New Orleans; and in a number of lake and river ports. Reportedly, syphilis and consumption accounted for more than one-half of the sailors treated.

THE US PUBLIC HEALTH Service traces its origins to the Act for the Relief of Sick and Disabled Seamen, passed in 1798 during the presidency of John Adams. Funded primarily through a tax of 20 cents a month on the salaries of sailors, the legislation provided for a number of marine hospitals dedicated to the care of disabled seamen.

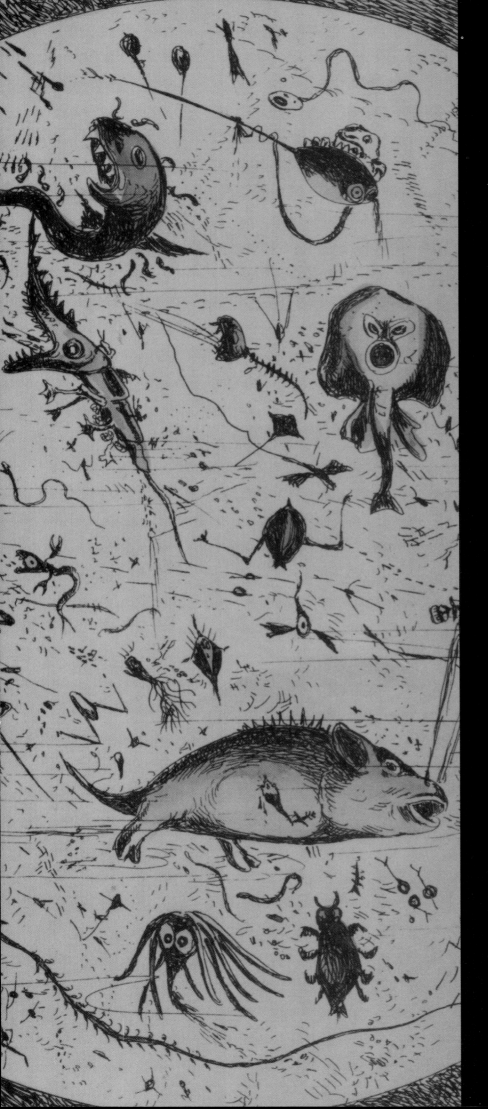

Chapter 2

" *M*onster **Soup** Commonly Called Thames Water" was one British cartoonist's rendering of London's *foul* **water** quality.

The Age
of Miasmas

1 8 0 0   t o   1 8 5 9

Little about the practical treatment of **infectious diseases** changed in America during the first half of the 19th century. Without the scientific tools to prove conclusively that diseases were transmitted from person to person—a theory promulgated by the "contagionists"—communicable diseases remained mysterious phenomena, striking universal fear in the hearts of most Americans and carrying thousands to untimely deaths with seeming unpredictability. Still, several important advances were made in the theoretical underpinnings of medical knowledge and would in time bear fruit.

First, the foundations of modern public hygiene were laid in Germany with the work of Johann Peter Frank. Frank's writings underscored the relationship between citizens' health and the nation's economic and political vitality, giving rise to greater activism by government officials in such matters as licensing doctors, the creation of city health agencies, and the institution of stricter quarantine laws. The use of statistics to systematically analyze and quantify social phenomena, from birth statistics and the comparative efficacy of various medical treatments to the causes of death, also came into use. Statistics provided the crucial first step in creating a new science of epidemiology. At the same time, a variety of instruments were adopted, including the thermometer, stethoscope, and laryngoscope, permitting physicians to investigate hidden regions and systems of the body.

Another breakthrough in medical thought can be traced to the Bostonian physician-teacher Oliver Wendell Holmes. In 1844, Dr. Holmes published a paper on puerperal fever in which he theorized that the virtual epidemic of deaths occurring among women immediately following obstetrical delivery was attributable to infections passed by their physicians. Working on this assumption, Holmes urged his colleagues to be scrupulous in washing hands and changing clothes between procedures. Holmes' unorthodox ideas were confirmed independently four years later in Europe by Ignaz Semmelweis.

The Holmes-Semmelweis theory coincided with the rise of the sanitary movement generally. Based upon an anticontagionist theory that health and disease were responses to environmental conditions, the sanitarians cited earthly emanations or "miasmas" as the chief offenders. As foul airs were typically associated with dirty streets, dank over-crowded housing, and the casual disposal of wastes such as existed in urban slums, the destitute and ill-housed immigrants who made up the bulk of America's poor and diseased were widely blamed for causing the epidemics. Clashes between resident populations and the alien newcomers were common, and newspapers kept up a steady barrage of hostile stories and satirical cartoons to feed the public's fears.

The connection between water and disease transmission was first identified by Dr. John Snow, a British pioneer in the new science of epidemiology.

The sanitary movement also found support in the work of Florence Nightingale, who led a small contingent of women volunteers to Turkey in 1854 to tend her countrymen in the field hospitals of the Crimean War. Nightingale's impassioned writings brought to public attention for the first time the filthy conditions in which men were housed and cared for in battle. Though she, too, blamed the high rate of deaths from disease on "miasmas," she made persuasive arguments for better hygiene in army barracks and hospitals. Nightingale exercised a powerful influence, particularly among reform-minded women in the United States, and would have a positive impact during the Civil War.

One of the most important antidotes to "miasmas," and vital to genuine disease prevention, was cleaning up the public water supply. The connection between water and disease transmission was first identified by Dr. John Snow, a British pioneer in the new science of epidemiology. Observing a series of horrifying outbreaks of Asian cholera, a disease making its first appearance in the West in 1832, Snow began to track the specific incidence of infection within particular communities. He came to suspect that the public water supply was somehow responsible. Londoners, for example, drew from a system that originated in the Thames River, the same water course that carried away untreated street, industrial, and household wastes. In hot, dry spells, when people were at their thirstiest and least likely to take water without boiling, the water delivered at neighborhood pumps was odorous, cloudy, and full of tiny creatures. Snow eventually prevailed upon the authorities to overhaul the city's sanitation and water supply, and the incidence of cholera and of typhoid declined in England. Similar improvements followed in many US cities, with the construction of public reservoirs and aqueducts bringing some relief.

Still, despite these reforms, epidemics continued to devastate many parts of the country, though the geographical distribution of some diseases began to change. Notably, yellow fever, which had plagued the Colonies for over a century, virtually disappeared from the Northeast after 1806 but became an almost yearly threat along the Southern Atlantic and Gulf coasts, reaching its peak just prior to the Civil War. Particularly hard hit were the port cities of Charleston, Savannah, and New Orleans, all entry points for the slave trade and centers of commerce chiefly with other tropical ports. Citizens were at risk of infection every time a new ship entered the harbor. Malaria, while less deadly, was another disease threatening the health of Southerners living in lowland areas especially.

Asiatic cholera also reached North America in the pandemic of 1832, attacking at many points along the eastern seaboard and making its way overland to the Pacific Coast by 1834. A second pandemic began in 1852, reaching its most virulent stage in 1854.

In terms of sheer frequency of epidemics, however, smallpox appeared more often than any other disease, with 14 major outbreaks over the century. Though protection was available both through the risky mode of "variolation" and with Edward Jenner's much safer cowpox "vaccination" introduced to the United States in 1800, neither measure gained widespread use here for many years. One physician's attempt to monopolize production of the Jenner vaccine, and a series of unfortunate accidents that left some of the vaccinated still vulnerable to infection were just a few of the problems. However, it was the prevailing ignorance of physicians and the public as to the true nature of infectious diseases that continued to be the largest obstacle to progress in this disease and the many others at large.

AN

INQUIRY

INTO

T·HE CAUSES AND EFFECTS

OF

THE VARIOLÆ VACCINÆ,

A DISEASE

DISCOVERED IN SOME OF THE WESTERN COUNTIES OF ENGLAND,

PARTICULARLY

GLOUCESTERSHIRE,

AND KNOWN BY THE NAME OF

THE COW POX.

BY EDWARD JENNER, M.D. F.R.S. &c.

————— QUID NOBIS CERTIUS IPSIS
SENSIBUS ESSE POTEST, QUO VERA AC FALSA NOTEMUS.
LUCRETIUS.

London:

PRINTED, FOR THE AUTHOR,

BY SAMPSON LOW, Nº. 7, BERWICK STREET, SOHO:

AND SOLD BY LAW, AVE-MARIA LANE; AND MURRAY AND HIGHLEY, FLEET STREET.

1798.

UNTIL THE PUBLICATION OF EDWARD JENNER'S *Inquiry* in 1798, the only known protection against smallpox was variolation. This involved implanting a small amount of infected matter from an active smallpox pustule into the skin of a healthy individual, and it generally brought on a mild case of smallpox resulting in lifetime immunity. But variolation was not entirely predictable: in roughly one-tenth of cases, the patient caught a full-scale infection and died. Jenner's method was infinitely safer. He came to it after observing that dairymaids rarely contracted smallpox. He concluded that the young women gained their immunity through contact with cows, among which a benign eruptive disease known as cowpox was endemic. Jenner presented his findings after experimenting with a procedure he called "vaccination" from the Latin *vaccinus*, pertaining to cows. In some countries vaccination soon became widespread, particularly as a means of protecting armies on the move. It was introduced into the United States as early as 1800 by Harvard professor Dr. Benjamin Waterhouse, shown above, using vaccine procured in London. It would take several decades for vaccination to become common practice among the general population of the United States. The detail (right) from Jenner's *Inquiry*, shows the appearance of a pustule following infection.

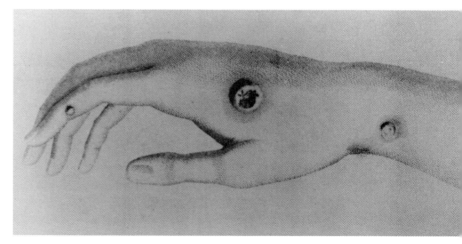

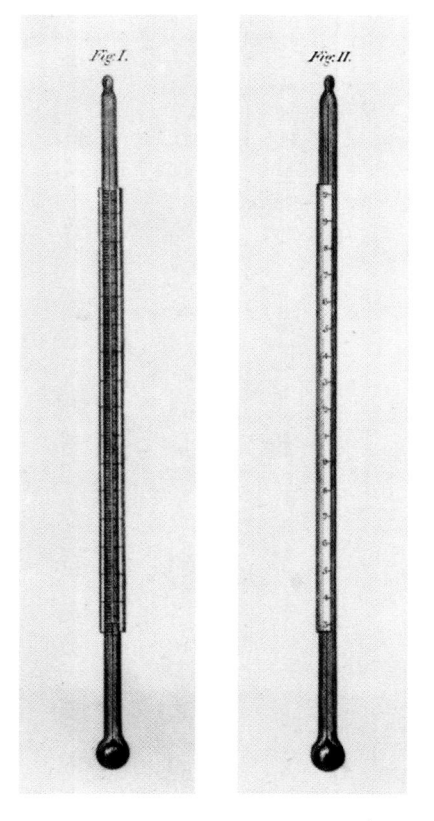

A CRITICAL ASPECT IN UNDERSTANDING the nature of infectious diseases lies in the clinician's ability to recognize and track symptoms. For much of human history, clinical observation had been restricted to reading the externals and studying cadavers. Body temperature, especially fever, was thought to be significant from an early period, but tools to make scientific measurements were late in coming. One of the first physicians to explain and recommend the use of a thermometer in clinical practice was Englishman John Hunter, regarded as the founder of experimental pathology. Hunter included this illustration in his classic text, *On Venereal Disease*, 1786. Thermometers did not come into common use until several decades later, however, when the German physician Karl Wunderlich wrote an exhaustive treatise on the relationship between body heat and disease. The compact and efficient design of the modern mercury thermometer came still later, in 1870.

ANOTHER STEP IN IMPROVING DIAGNOSTIC abilities was introduced in 1761 when the Viennese physician Leopold Auenbrugger developed a technique called percussion, which involved thumping the chest and listening to different tones to determine the status of organs and tumors. Auenbrugger's work remained little known until 1808 when it was translated into French by Jean-Nicolas Corvisart. His student, René-Theophile Hyacinthe Laënnec, went on to expand upon the principle with his invention of the stethoscope and a procedure he called "mediate oscultation." Laënnec's first instrument was a rolled tube of paper, his next a hollow wooden device. Still later versions named for other inventors featured various segmented tubes and detachable chest and ear pieces. This illustration is taken from an 1869 catalogue and shows a number of different monaural models, Laënnec's among them.

STETHOSCOPES.

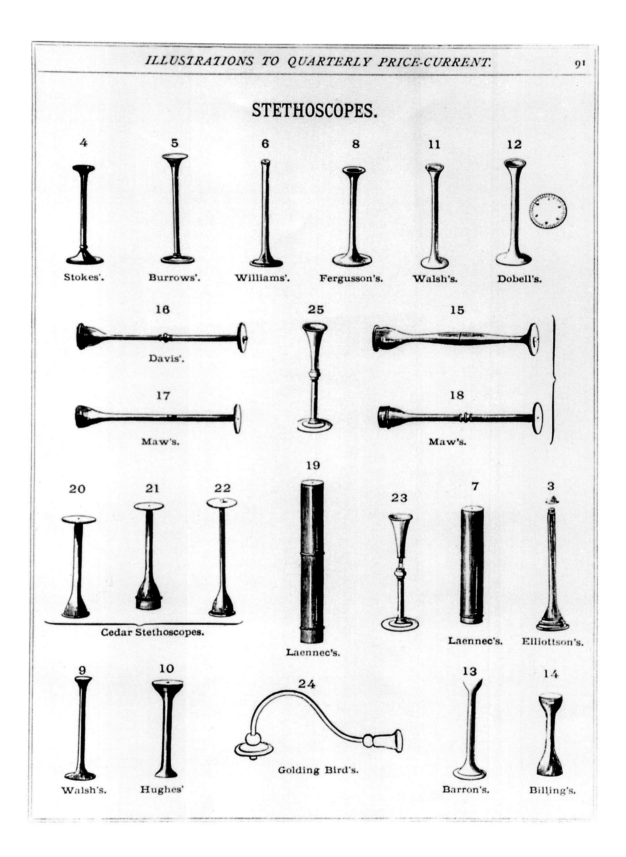

OLIVER WENDELL HOLMES, best known as a genial essayist, was the first physician to recognize the contagious nature of puerperal fever. Despite publication of a paper on the subject in 1843, Holmes was unable to persuade many of his colleagues to improve their hygienic practices. Then, in 1847, Viennese obstetrician Ignaz Semmelweis used the new science of statistical evidence to uncover patterns of puerperal fever outbreak among patients in the maternity ward of his hospital. He found that women who came down with childbed fever were typically those who had been visited by medical students on their rounds. By contrast, new mothers who were tended by midwives rarely became infected. The critical difference he observed was in the sanitary practices of the two attending groups: unlike the midwives, who routinely washed their hands with soap and water before and after delivering, the medical students rarely did so; appearing at bedsides with the blood of previous patients on their hands, they literally carried disease from patient to patient. Thus was born the concept of asepsis, in which physicians gradually adopted such simple practices as boiling water and scrubbing hands in an attempt to create a germ-free environment. Medical instruments (right), like the early scarifier, were also sterilized with greater frequency, though rubber gloves and fresh surgical gowns would not become a common feature of the operating room for many decades to come.

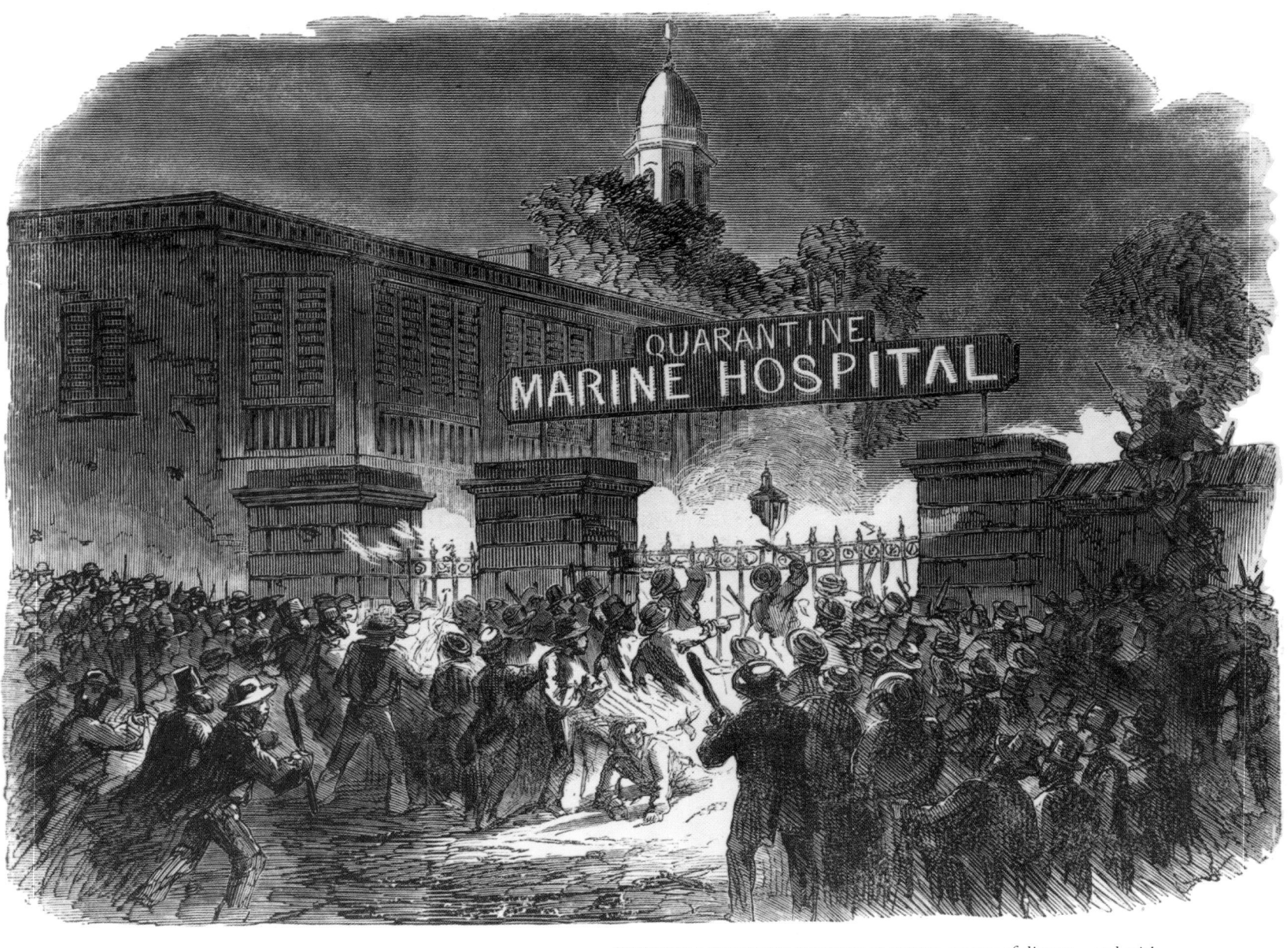

CITIES WERE INCREASINGLY REGARDED AS POTENT centers of disease—and with
good reason. Epidemics were capable of traveling with impunity in
crowded urban environments. Nowhere was this more a problem than
in US port cities, where never-ending waves of immigrants brought new
strains of Old World diseases into populations that from an immunologic
point of view were relatively virginal. The illustration above, from an
1858 issue of *Harper's Weekly*, depicts an attack on the Marine Hospital
located on Staten Island in New York harbor. An angry mob sacked the
facility because yellow-fever patients were being landed and detained
there. Concern was that the hospital and its occupants were "breeding
pestilence," threatening the entire population. The same isolationist
sentiment is expressed in the engraving (right) depicting the Angel of
Cleanliness, who bars the gate against the cringing demons of cholera,
yellow fever, and smallpox.

PUBLIC WATER SUPPLIES GRADUALLY EMERGED as one of the prime sources of disease transmission. "Monster Soup Commonly Called Thames Water" was one British cartoonist's rendering of London's foul water quality. The artist anticipated by more than two decades the findings of John Snow, who reported in 1849 that cholera was a waterborne disease, and that much of London's drinking water was casually polluted by sewage that contained a variety of disease organisms. Called in to find out why Londoners on the south side of the river were more prone to developing cholera than the people in the rest of the city, Snow found that the water being delivered to the St. James district via its communal Broad Street pump was particularly virulent. His practical solution was to remove the pump's handle, forcing citizens to go elsewhere until the water company improved its filtration system.

MICROCOSM · dedicated to the Londo

MONSTER SOUP commonly called

Pub by J McLean 26 Haymarket

MONSTER SOUP commonly called THAMES WATER, being a correct representation of that precious stuff doled out to us !!!

Water Companies , BROUGHT FORTH ALL MONSTROUS, ALL PRODIGIOUS THINGS, HYDRAS, AND GORGONS, AND CHIMERAS DIRE. Vide Milton

titled by other Caricatures are daily Published the largest collection of any house in Town

CONCERNS OVER WATER QUALITY prompted
many American municipalities to clean up
their delivery systems. The Croton Reservoir,
shown above, stood in the middle of New
York City and was fed via an elaborate
aqueduct system from crystal-clear streams
well to the north of the metropolis.
Completed in 1842, the system was a
source of municipal pride. "Nothing is
talked or thought of in New York but
Croton water," wrote one diarist with
evident pride.

AS MUCH OF 19TH-CENTURY MEDICAL treatment proved ineffective against diseases, doctors were common butts of stinging satire. In this engraving by Thomas Rowlandson, physicians were depicted as charlatans, profiting from disease. Other cartoonists suggested that doctors actually planted disease in the population to increase business, though records indicate that mortality due to diseases was at least as high among doctors as it was in the general population, and often higher.

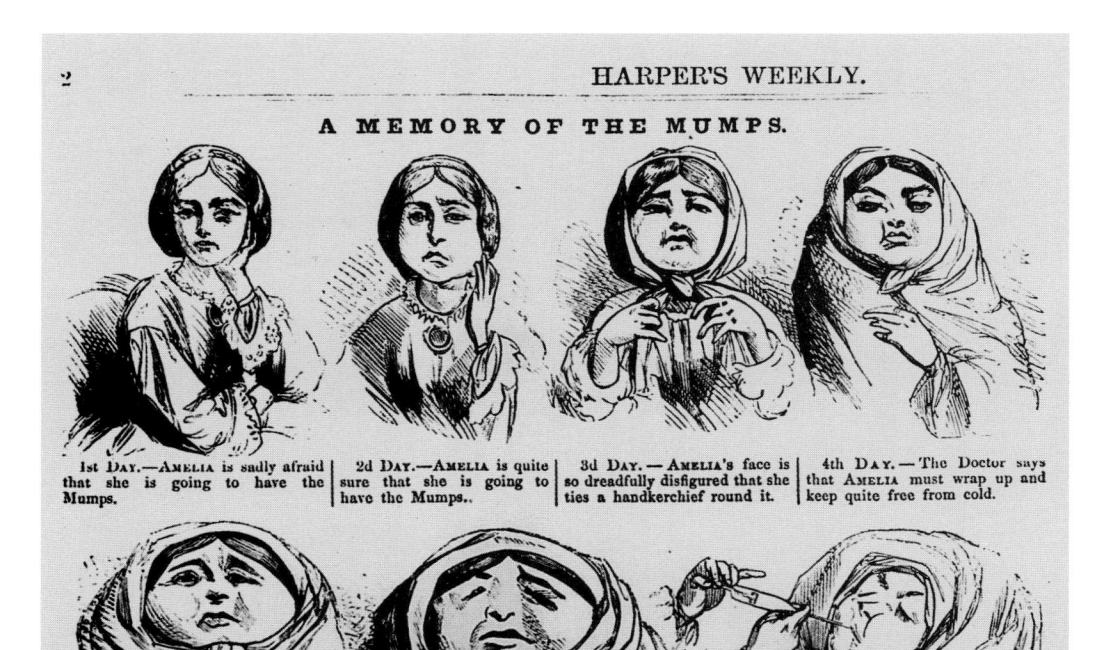

A MEMORY OF THE MUMPS.

1st Day.—Amelia is sadly afraid that she is going to have the Mumps.

2d Day.—Amelia is quite sure that she is going to have the Mumps..

3d Day.—Amelia's face is so dreadfully disfigured that she ties a handkerchief round it.

4th Day.—The Doctor says that Amelia must wrap up and keep quite free from cold.

5th Day.—Amelia looks in the glass and can not recognize herself.

6th Day.—Amelia hopes to goodness that dear Frederick will not see her.

7th Day.—Amelia's mouth being hermetically sealed, she is obliged to be fed through a quill.—N. B. After this the subject becomes too horrible for representation.

MUMPS WAS ONE OF THE FIRST childhood epidemic diseases to be recognized as a unique entity, and its description appears in the writings of Hippocrates. But perhaps because its potential to develop into a more serious secondary disease was not recognized, or because its agent, a virus, was not known until the 20th century, mumps received relatively little serious attention. Here, in an illustration from *Harper's Weekly*, it is treated as a comical event, a temporary source of disfigurement during the maneuverings of one young couple's courtship.

THOUGH HARDLY A MATCH for the apocalyptic diseases, the common cold was given its due in popular literature in the 19th century. This 1846 lithograph by Currier & Ives shows that hot soup has a long tradition as a reliable remedy.

GOOD FOR A COLD.

CHOLERA, BY CONTRAST, was a major killer in the 19th century. Unknown in Europe in previous centuries, this epidemic diarrheal disease swept out of Asia in 1817 and within a decade came knocking on the doors of Western Europe. Causing extensive misery and loss of life there, it subsequently leapt the Atlantic, purportedly entering North America and the port of New York via an Irish immigrant family in 1832. Like the majority of those infected in the pre-antibiotic era, the infected father, mother, and two children died within a week of exhibiting their first symptoms. From New York, cholera radiated outward, traveling rivers, canals, coastal waterways, and roads along with human migrations. Here, passengers prostrate with cholera suffer below decks in the steerage cabin that they share with livestock aboard a Mississippi River steamer.

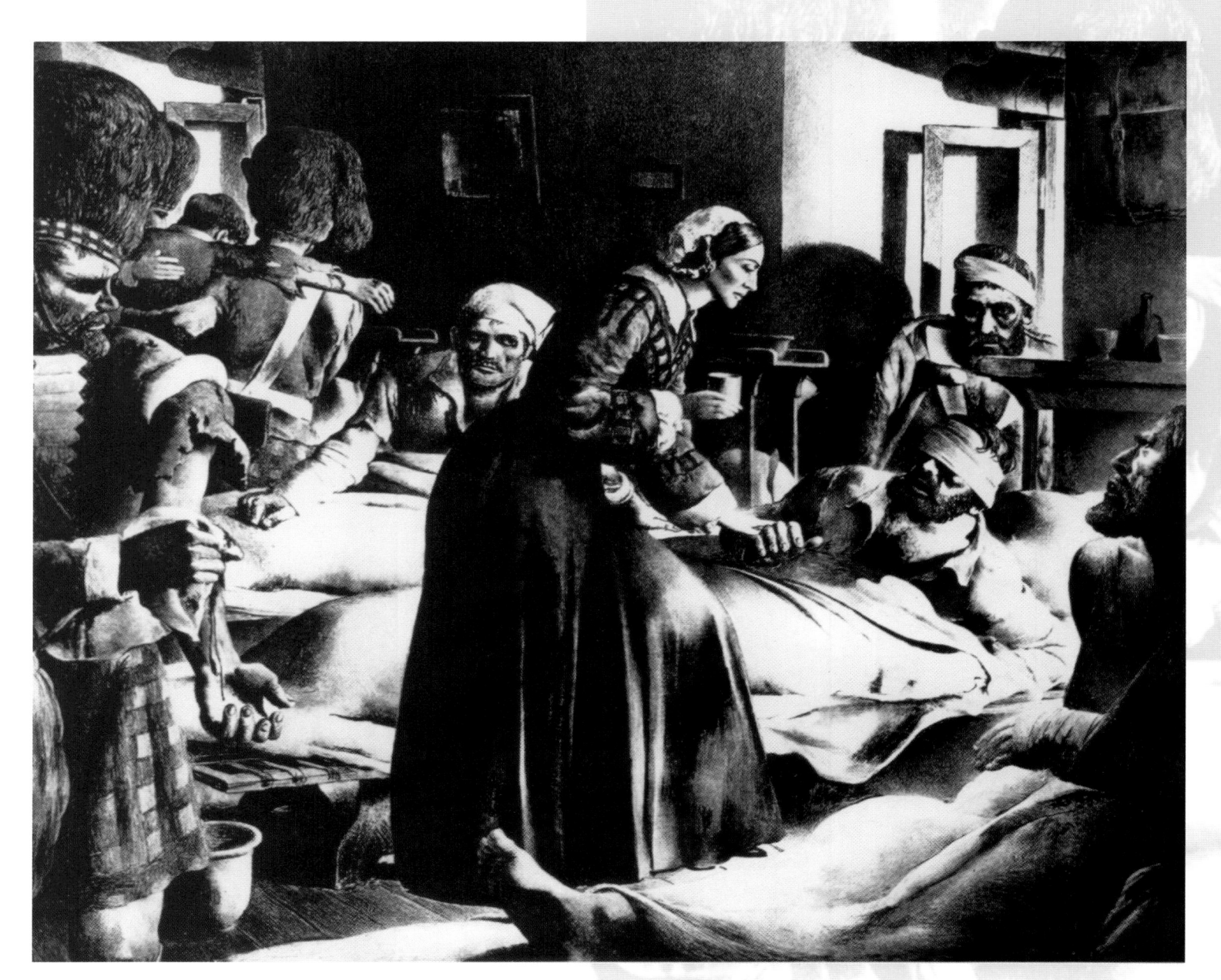

FLORENCE NIGHTINGALE is widely credited not only with changing
nursing from a casual endeavor to a profession but with having
reinvented the design of hospital wards in the latter half of the
19th century. Nightingale developed her ideas in 1854 during the
Crimean War when she led a small corps of nurses to a demoralized
barracks hospital in Scutari, Turkey, to treat the British wounded.
Before her arrival, mortality rates were running over 40% from
disease and infection alone. At one point, the hospital water supply
was found to be flowing over the body of a dead horse! Though
Nightingale never came to believe in the physical existence of
germs, she was compulsive about the importance of cleanliness,
adequate nutrition, good ventilation, pure water, and efficient
drainage as critical to patient health. Within three months of her
arrival in the Crimea, as her theories were put to practical test,
mortality rates plummeted. She is shown here in a painting by
Riggs tending the sick and wounded.

THE LANCET, an ancient device for opening and draining lesions, evolved over time into a tool for administering vaccines. Small cuts were made in the skin, after which infective materials capable of producing an immune response were bound into the wound. The spring lancet shown was an advance over the ordinary blade knife in that it gave the physician greater control over the length and depth of the wound.

Chapter 3

*T*he grim **conditions suffered** by combatants in war have been described many times, but what is not often said is that up to World War II **infectious diseases** caused far more deaths than **battle injuries**.

The Age
of Bacteriology

1 8 6 0   t o   1 8 9 3

The grim **conditions suffered by combatants** in war have been described many times, but what is not often said is that up to World War II infectious diseases caused far more deaths than battle injuries. The American Civil War was a tragic case in point. By the reckoning of the Confederate Army's Medical Inspector, roughly three times as many Southern combatants died of acute disease as were brought down by rifle or sword; the record of the North was only slightly better. All told, perhaps 375 000 Americans in their prime died of infections of one sort or another during the four years of civil warfare. Still more men fell ill but ultimately recovered sufficiently to go home. In this welter of sickness and suffering, the medical profession found itself only slightly better prepared than the British had been in the previous decade during the Crimean War.

The reasons for the terrible disease toll of this and other wars were simple. Many of the Civil War combatants came from isolated rural communities where they might escape the milder childhood encounters with chickenpox, diphtheria, measles, mumps, scarlet fever, and whooping cough. But thrown together in the tight communities of fighting men, under poor sanitary conditions and high levels of stress, and lacking acquired immunity to such diseases, they were easy marks for one infection after another. Measles, in particular, spread like wildfire through the camps, often crossing battle lines to fell hundreds at a time. Smallpox also traveled widely, despite belated efforts to vaccinate troops. Typhoid, malaria, dysentery, and pulmonary diseases—chiefly, tuberculosis—also stalked the exhausted and injured.

At the tented field hospitals, conditions were scarcely better than those in the dreaded prison camps. Volunteers of the US Sanitary Commission, primarily women anxious to emulate the work of Nightingale and her sisters, did their best to raise hygienic standards, but a wounded man's chances of surviving in such places remained poor indeed. One ailing Union soldier wrote home that he preferred to go back to fighting than to go see an army doctor, "thinking that I had better die by rebel bullets than Union quackery." At the larger base hospitals, which were thrown up behind the lines in several locations, a new "pavilion" model of architecture was followed. The pavilion style offered high ceilings, oversized windows, east-west exposure, and superior ventilation, thought to be the best defense against miasmal infection. Pavilion wards typically radiated around a common treatment center, making it possible to segregate the otherwise healthy wounded from the infected as a prudent measure to reduce contagion.

Pasteurization, as the sterilization process became known, was particularly important in controlling the spread of tuberculosis infection via the milk of tubercular cows.

Meanwhile, in Europe, several key investigations were underway that would simultaneously launch the new "era of bacteriology" and further improve physicians' ability to diagnose and differentiate diseases. In France, chemist Louis Pasteur carried out a series of brilliant studies laying the empirical foundations for the germ theory of disease. First, he proved that living organisms rather than vague miasmas or spontaneously generated inert chemicals were responsible for the fermentation that altered wine, beer, milk, and many other substances. He went on to show that these organisms were typically in greatest concentrations in the air of warm rooms and the polluted atmosphere of cities, and that the best means of getting rid of them was exposure to high heat. Pasteurization, as the sterilization process became known, was particularly important in controlling the spread of tuberculosis infection via the milk of tubercular cows. Pasteur also developed vaccines for chicken cholera and anthrax, discoveries that prepared the way for the development of the first rabies vaccine, which he produced in 1884.

With the existence of microscopic germs and some of their actions firmly established, Glasgow surgeon Joseph Lister undertook an all-out attack against the septicemia and gangrene associated with surgery. In 1865, Lister introduced an operating technique that involved bathing the surgical area in an antiseptic misting of weak carbolic acid. And in Berlin, physician Robert

From Wunderlich's time forward, physicians used body temperature as one of the more reliable measures of charting disease process.

Koch put the germ theory on a firm scientific foundation by first developing techniques for obtaining pure cultures and staining pathogenic bacteria. He went on to formulate a set of criteria, the famed "Koch's postulates," by which one could establish an absolute connection between particular pathogens and particular diseases. Koch climaxed this grand work by isolating the "germs" of anthrax, tuberculosis, and cholera.

Another important contribution to the understanding of disease came from fellow German Karl Wunderlich, whose classic *Temperature in Diseases*, published in Leipzig in 1868, used the data collected from 25 000 patients to chart the relationship of fever to acute infection. From Wunderlich's time forward, physicians used body temperature as one of the more reliable measures of charting disease process.

Despite these impressive breakthroughs in scientific understanding in the latter half of the 19th century, American medicine continued to lag well behind Europe, in putting the information into practice. (The preferred methods of dealing with infectious diseases in the United States remained quarantine, improved sanitation, and moral uplift.) Americans also proved highly receptive to patent medicines and unorthodox technology, putting their faith and health in all forms of odd elixirs and buzzing electrical devices, the more spectacular the better.

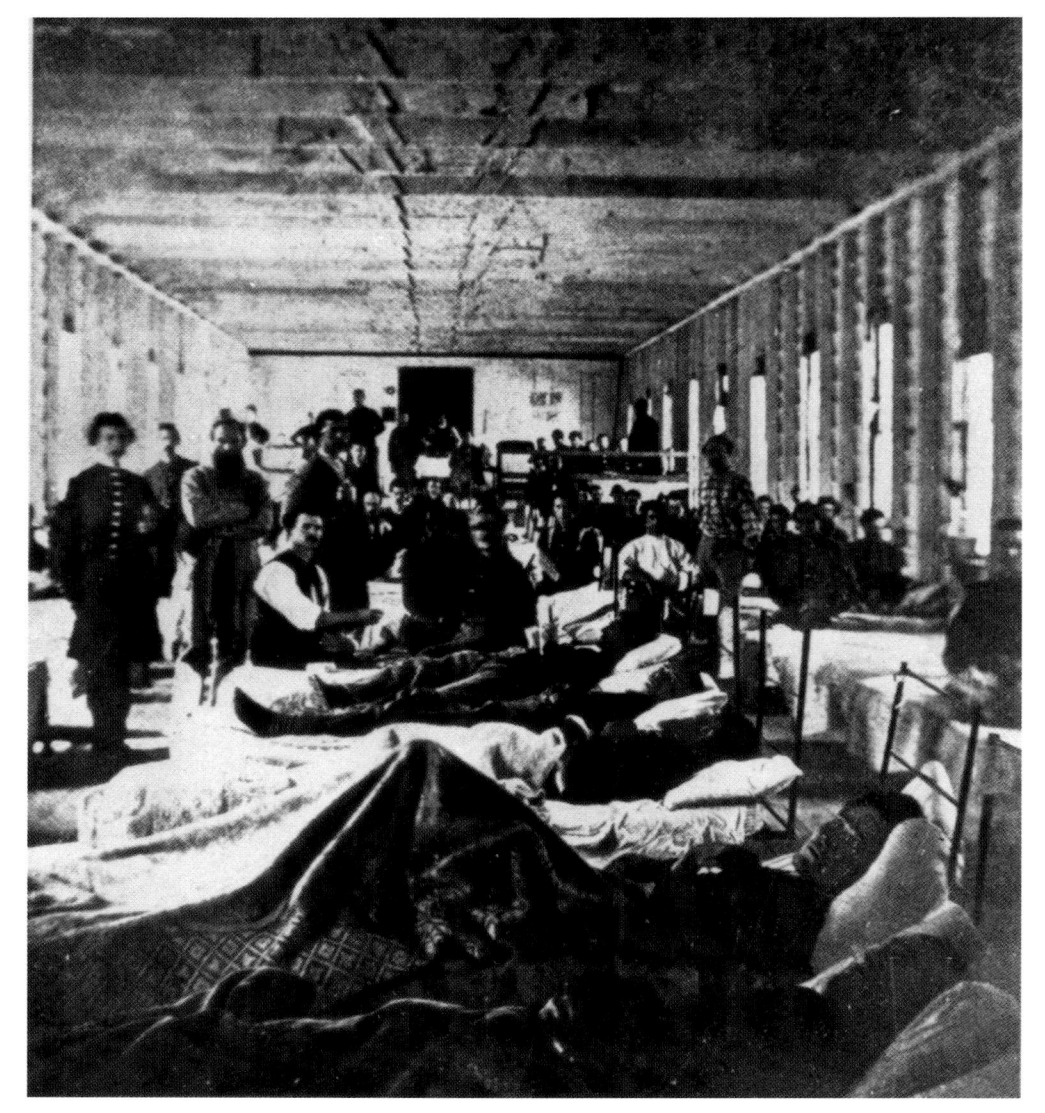

WOUNDED VETERANS pass the hours in the bright, sunny spaces of Armory Square Hospital, another temporary facility constructed by the Union Army. Generously sized windows, sparkling white walls, and floors of hardwood, their seams filled with paraffin and the surfaces polished, were all thought to improve the sanitary conditions as well as morale of patients and medical personnel.

LINCOLN HOSPITAL, constructed in Washington, DC, for the care of the wounded and sick of the Civil War, demonstrated many of the features of modern design first elaborated by Florence Nightingale. Rather than crowding many men together in airless spaces, the newer, more progressive facilities sorted patients according to their disease, keeping them in designated tents—one for typhoid, another for measles, another for pneumonia, and so on. As the numbers of battle wounded mounted, Lincoln Hospital became a small city in its complexity and size, covering 16 acres and containing 34 wards and 4500 beds. Still, the medical knowledge underlying patient care remained fairly primitive and "miasmic odors" were blamed for a substantial share of the disease fatalities.

THE TASK OF NURSING THE SICK of the Civil War fell chiefly to women volunteers. The famed writer Louisa May Alcott wrote of her "somewhat abrupt plunge" into nursing as an unsettling experience. Evidently, the ward to which she was first assigned was not as progressively managed as Lincoln, for there was no attempt to segregate patients according to disease. Alcott wrote, "I spent my shining hours washing faces, serving rations, giving medicine, and sitting in a very hard chair, with pneumonia on one side, diphtheria on the other, five typhoids on the opposite, and a dozen dilapidated patriots, hopping, lying and lounging about."

FRENCH CHEMIST LOUIS PASTEUR first devised the process of decontamination known as "pasteurization" (partial heat sterilization) as a means of deterring fermentation in wine. It was soon applied with excellent results to beer and milk, and still later to human bacteria, or "microbes" as Pasteur dubbed them. His studies also showed for the first time that microorganisms were not the effect of disease but the cause of it, and that they occur not through spontaneous generation but through "small corpuscles" living in the environment, many of them reaching the site of infection by air. Pasteur, pictured here in an 1885 portrait, went on to lay the foundation of the science of immunology through his investigations of attenuated infective agents, and to develop vaccines against anthrax, rabies, and swine erysipelas. His world-famous Pasteur Institute, which opened in Paris in 1888, became a center for the study of immunology.

But the boy lived and was perfectly healthy. The remedy for hydrophobia had been found.

PASTEUR'S DISCOVERY OF AN EFFECTIVE VACCINE against rabies, or hydrophobia as it was often termed, marked a milestone in the history of immunization. He began a concentrated study of the disease in 1880, developing an attenuated and predictable vaccine to protect dogs in 1884. A year later, with some trepidation, he applied his discovery to Joseph Meister, a nine-year-old boy from Alsace. Meister, who had received 14 bites from a mad dog, was sent to Pasteur by his local doctor in a desperate attempt to save him from certain death. Given a series of increasingly potent rabies' inoculations over a two-week period, young Meister made a complete recovery. News of Pasteur's achievement brought him some 2500 additional patients in the next 18 months, and all but 10 of these survived. Typical of the range of vaccinating devices used by Pasteur's contemporaries in America are the devices shown, taken from a catalog of George Tiemann & Company, published in 1889.

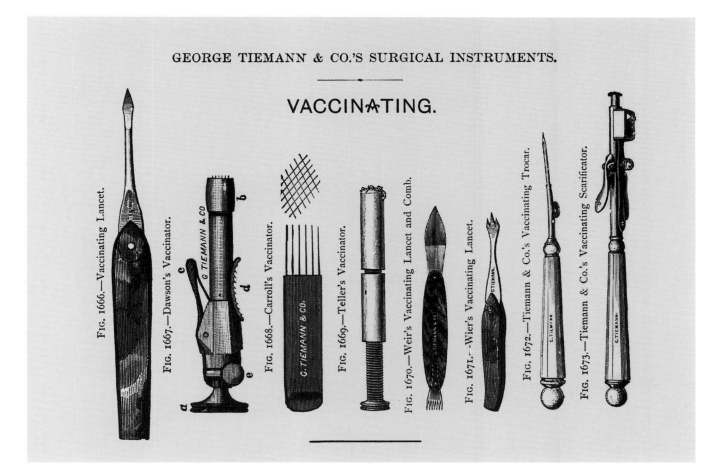

GEORGE TIEMANN & CO.'S SURGICAL INSTRUMENTS.

VACCINATING.

FIG. 1666.—Vaccinating Lancet.

FIG. 1667.—Dawson's Vaccinator.

FIG. 1668.—Carroll's Vaccinator.

FIG. 1669.—Teller's Vaccinator.

FIG. 1670.—Weir's Vaccinating Lancet and Comb.

FIG. 1671.—Wier's Vaccinating Lancet.

FIG. 1672.—Tiemann & Co.'s Vaccinating Trocar.

FIG. 1673.—Tiemann & Co.'s Vaccinating Scarificator.

Lord Lister (1827 - 1912)
BARRAUD & JERRARD

SCOTTISH PROFESSOR OF SURGERY JOSEPH LISTER
came to his interest in antisepsis as the
result of his concern over the high mortality
rate following surgical amputations. Despite
Lister's best efforts to keep wounds clean,
45% of his cases ended in fatality. He
ultimately determined that septicemia
and hospital gangrene were connected with
a process of rotting tissue, and this led him
to read a paper by Louis Pasteur on the
topic of anaerobic fermentation. Lister concluded that microorganisms might enter a
wound via the air, and he devised a method
of killing these invaders with a disinfectant
chemical. His paper describing his pioneer-
ing methods was published in the *Lancet*
in 1867, since regarded as the birth year
of antisepsis.

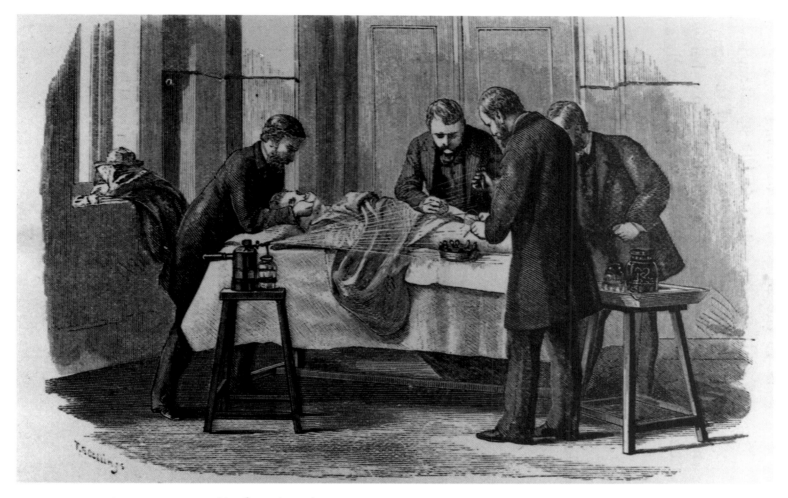

BEFORE LISTER'S TIME, everything from wine and vinegar to iodine, turpentine, and creosote had been tried as disinfectants with limited success. Lister favored carbolic acid, and in the wake of his discovery, various devices for misting the substance in the vicinity of the operating theater were invented. The diffuser shown here appeared in William Watson Cheyne's *Antiseptic Surgery*, 1882.

ROBERT KOCH (front row, fourth from left)
poses with students and faculty at the
conclusion of his first postgraduate course in
the new science of bacteriology. The group,
which comprised medical professionals
from all over the world, met at the newly
opened Institute for Infectious Diseases in
Berlin in 1891, nine years after publication
of Koch's landmark "postulates."

KOCH

CHOCOLAT GUÉRIN-BOUTRON

KOCH, médecin Allemand, né en 1843, découvre, en étudiant le choléra aux Indes, le bacille qui porte son nom, puis le bacille de la tuberculose, qui fait prévoir la guérison de cette maladie.

LES BIENFAITEURS DE L'HUMANITÉ

84 Sujets variés

Tuberculinu Kochii

KOCH IS CREDITED with having identified the bacillus responsible for tuberculosis. He followed this with the announcement in 1890 that he had found a remedy in a cure he called tuberculin, the glycerin extract of tubercle bacilli shown. Koch's latter claim proved premature, however, and many individuals died following treatment. But tuberculin proved valuable as a means of diagnosing tuberculosis in that it generated an allergic reaction in people already infected with the tuberculosis bacilli. So famous was Koch in his time that makers of patent medicines often borrowed his name to add luster to their products, as in the advertising card for a cholera and tuberculosis remedy.

BY THE MID 1870s, Joseph Lister's notions regarding the airborne transmission of germs had begun to have an impact on the physical design of hospitals. One of the most visible examples is seen in John Shaw Billings's 1875 design of Johns Hopkins Hospital's "Isolating Ward." The ward consisted of 20 private rooms for patients, each with its own exterior ventilation and chimney. Also included were accommodations for four nurses who would live in virtual quarantine for a week at a time to minimize the possibility of spreading disease. To further inhibit the spread of infection, walls were of double thickness, entry to each room was through two doors separated by a small vestibule, and individual waste closets with sanitizing steam coils were provided.

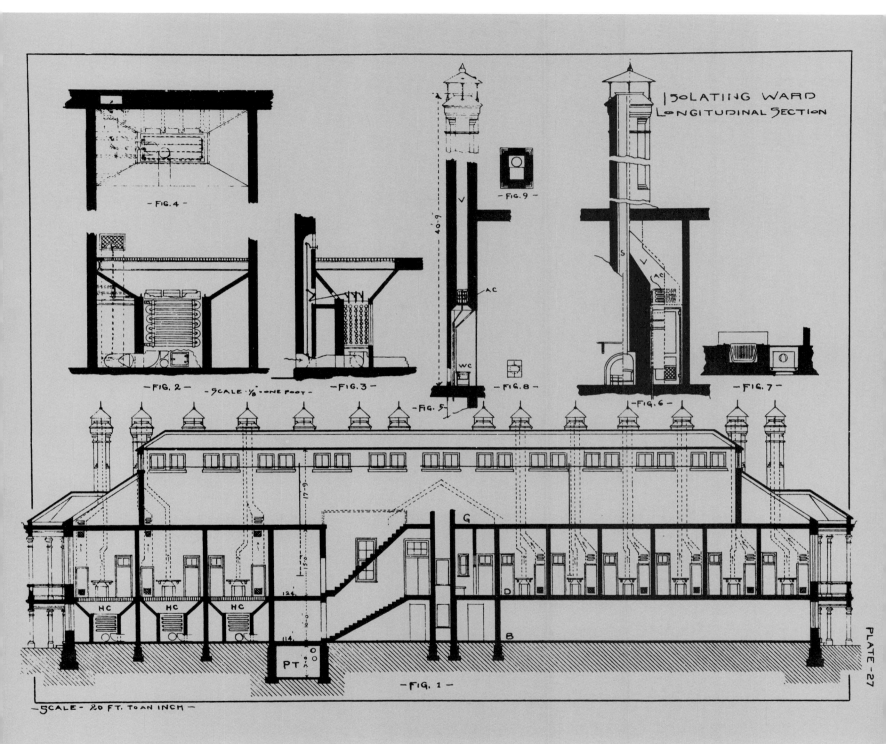

ISOLATING WARD
LONGITUDINAL SECTION

- FIG. 4 -

- FIG. 2 -   - SCALE ⅛ TO ONE FOOT -   - FIG. 3 -

- FIG. 9 -

- FIG. 5 -   - FIG. 8 -   - FIG. 6 -   - FIG. 7 -

- FIG. 1 -

- SCALE - 20 FT. TO AN INCH -

PLATE - 27

WASHINGTON, DC, while looking far tidier than New York City on the surface, had some serious problems from the public health standpoint as well. In this 1881 cartoon for *Harper's Weekly,* Thomas Nast satirizes the wide gap between the official view of the Capital's charms and the realities of actually living there. Since the city's founding, the daily conditions of all classes had been deplorable. Along with unpaved streets and underfunded sewage and garbage services, citizens had to cope with the excruciating heat of summer and the bad airs emanating from the drained swamps and lowlands that lay between the Potomac River and Tiber Creek. Malaria was the chief danger. Even as the gentleman reads this cheerful poster, he appears to be suffering from the early stages of malarial fever.

AS THE STUDIES OF PUBLIC HEALTH and environmental conditions grew more sophisticated, social workers and government officials began to look ever more closely at urban settlement patterns. New York's Tenth Ward had the distinction of being the most crowded slum district in the world in 1890 when this photo of Hester Street, popularly known as the "Pig-Market," was taken. Into these tenements human beings were packed more densely than anywhere else on record, the slums of China and India not excepted, with 522 people per acre estimated by the Bureau of Vital Statistics. Not surprisingly, the highest incidence of typhus and suicide was also recorded here.

THE QUARANTINE ACT OF 1893 transferred the authority for screening immigrants from state and local agencies to the federal government. With two-thirds of newcomers arriving aboard ships entering the Port of New York, the public health officers at Ellis Island had to screen as many as 5000 candidates each day as they made their way along "The Line." Left, a young Irish woman has her hair inspected for lice. At right, Jewish immigrants are required to strip to the waist to undergo chest examinations by public health officers. In another view, scores of immigrants in a large reception hall await an uncertain future as they prepare to undergo examination.

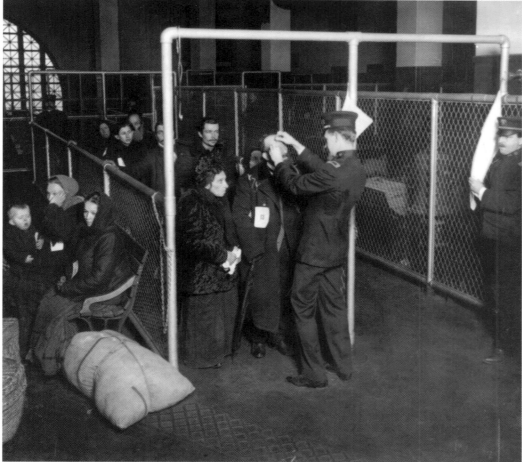

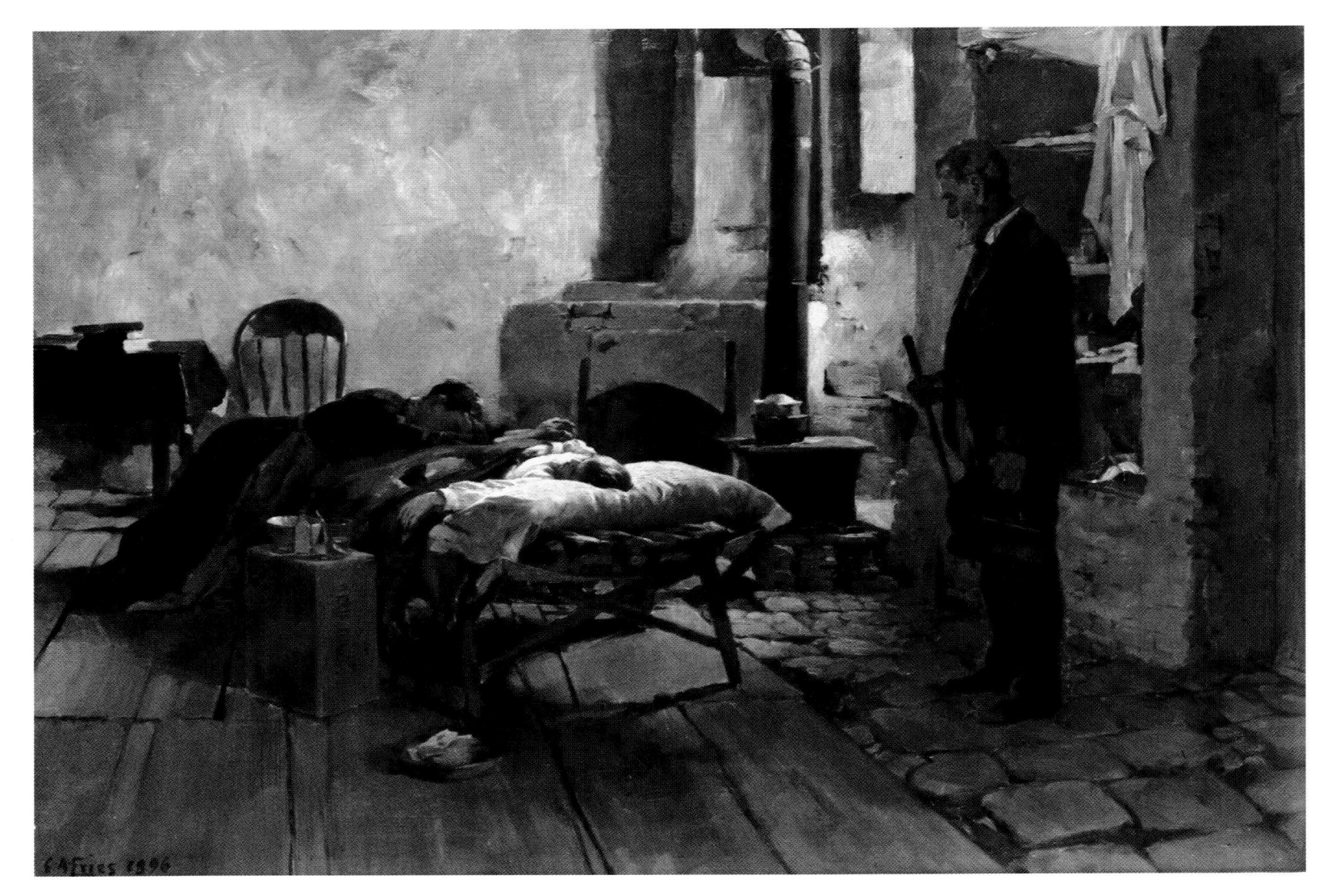

THE INCIDENCE OF PULMONARY TUBERCULOSIS, popularly known as "phthisis" or "consumption," peaked in the United States in the middle of the 19th century. And while its consequences were rightly feared, the disease was also associated with heightened sensibilities and creativity among the middle and upper classes. This gave rise to the frequent appearance of consumptives as subjects for romantic opera and painting. The "look" of consumption—pale, languorous, and wasted—was even adopted as an ideal of feminine beauty. Shown above is a classic depiction of the disease in its terminal phase. Titled "Too Late," the dramatic painting is by the American painter Charles Arthur Fries, 1896.

TUBERCULOSIS SPAWNED A HOST OF DEVICES designed to improve the breathing abilities of persons with compromised lung capacity. Shown above are a pair of hand-held inhalers manufactured by Codman & Shurtleff, Boston, 1890. The more elaborate inhalation devices, right, were among the offerings in the George Tiemann & Co. catalog, *American Armamentarium Chirurgicum*, published in 1889. Particularly intriguing was Franckel's pneumatic accordion, which when played by the tuberculosis patient caused alternately rarefied and condensed air to move through the lungs.

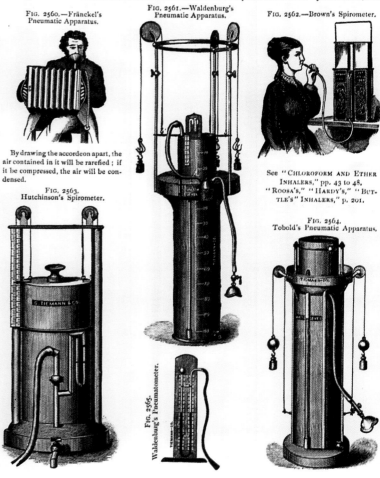

GEORGE TIEMANN & CO.'S SURGICAL INSTRUMENTS.

INHALERS.

Pneumatic Apparatus, for Inhalation of Condensed and Rarefied Air.

"In compressed and rarefied air we have powerful means of physically impressing the respiratory and circulatory systems, and thus of acting therapeutically upon them in diseases in which their functions are abnormally executed.

Inspiration of compressed air increases the pressure on the lungs, and thus augments the vital capacity; the chest becoming expanded to greater extent than can be accomplished by the most powerful voluntary inspiration of normal air. * * * *Expiration into compressed air* diminishes the quantity of expired air in proportion to the density of the compressed air."—"Inhalation in the Treatment of Disease: its Therapeutics and Practice." J. Solis Cohen, M.D.

FIG. 2560.—Fränckel's Pneumatic Apparatus.

FIG. 2561.—Waldenburg's Pneumatic Apparatus.

FIG. 2562.—Brown's Spirometer.

By drawing the accordeon apart, the air contained in it will be rarefied; if it be compressed, the air will be condensed.

See "CHLOROFORM AND ETHER INHALERS," pp. 43 to 48. "ROOSA'S," "HARDY'S," "BUTTLE'S" INHALERS," p. 201.

FIG. 2563. Hutchinson's Spirometer.

FIG. 2564. Tobold's Pneumatic Apparatus.

FIG. 2565. Waldenburg's Pneumatometer.

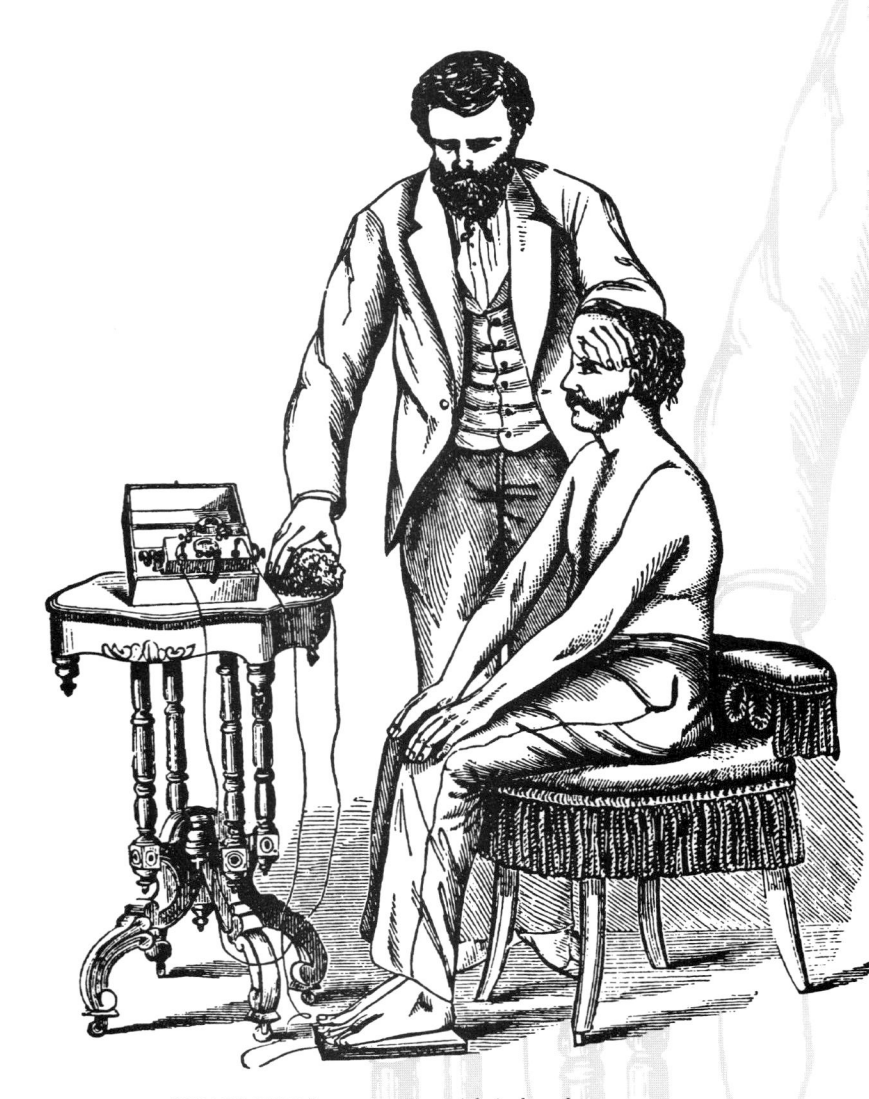

"FARADIZATION," a treatment with induced currents, was one of a class of electrotherapeutic modes used to treat consumption. In theory, low doses of electricity energized fatigued lungs as well as the nervous system generally. This illustration is taken from *Medical and Surgical Electricity*, 1878, a standard textbook on electrotherapy by the American physicians George Beard and Alphonse Recoil.

THE PULVERMACHER GALVANIC BELT, introduced in 1857, was one of scores of electrical devices offered for personal use. Made in Cleveland, it consisted of a network of very small batteries that, after being soaked in a saline solution, did in fact generate a weak electrical current. Its manufacturer claimed that the belt could cure "all nervous, chronic, and functional diseases." Particularly susceptible to the blandishments of advertisers were anxious young men who were led to believe that syphilis was everywhere. Still later, high-frequency currents were used to cure acute conjunctivitis, catarrh, yellow fever, and a condition known as "general debility." Another electrotherapeutic modality that enjoyed brief celebrity was hyperpyrexia, a risky procedure that induced an artificial fever sufficiently high to kill certain disease organisms. Dangerous at best, hyperpyrexia did show some success in treating venereal diseases, especially gonococcal infections.

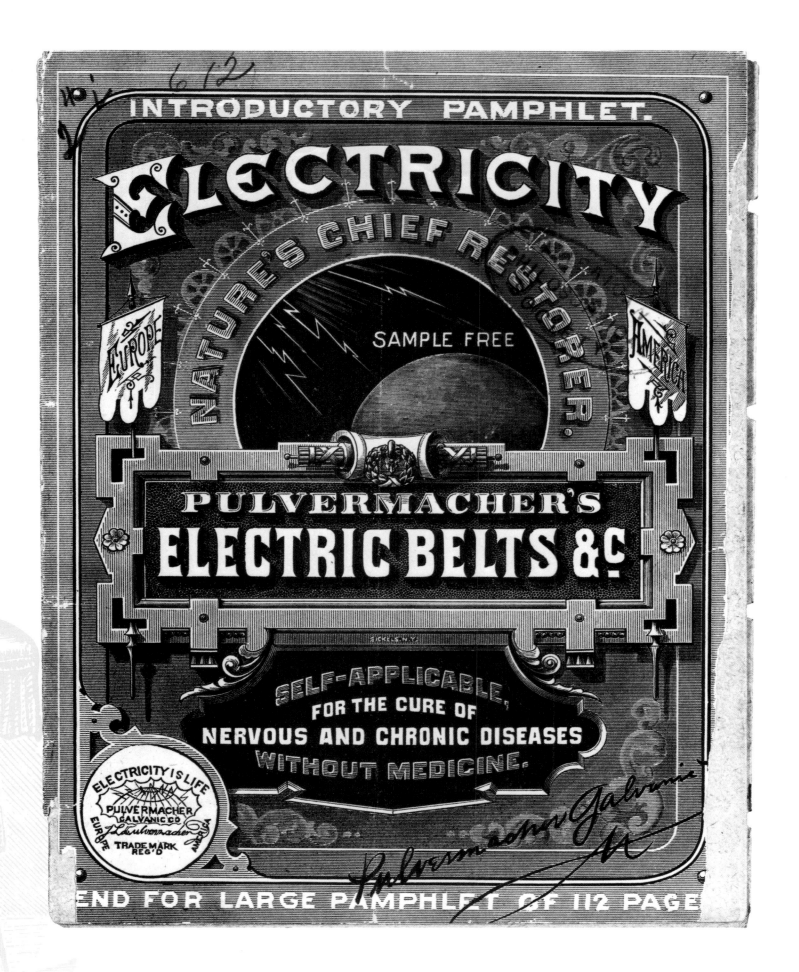

WHEN A YELLOW FEVER EPIDEMIC ERUPTED in 1888, the Marine Hospital Service detained persons suspected of harboring the disease at Camp E. A. Perry, near the Florida-Alabama border (above). That same year Surgeon-General George M. Sternberg localized "*Bacillus* X" in yellow fever, a prime first step to investigating its causes. Shown at left are three well-starched nurses employed by the Marine Hospital Service at a later outbreak of yellow fever in Franklin, Louisiana.

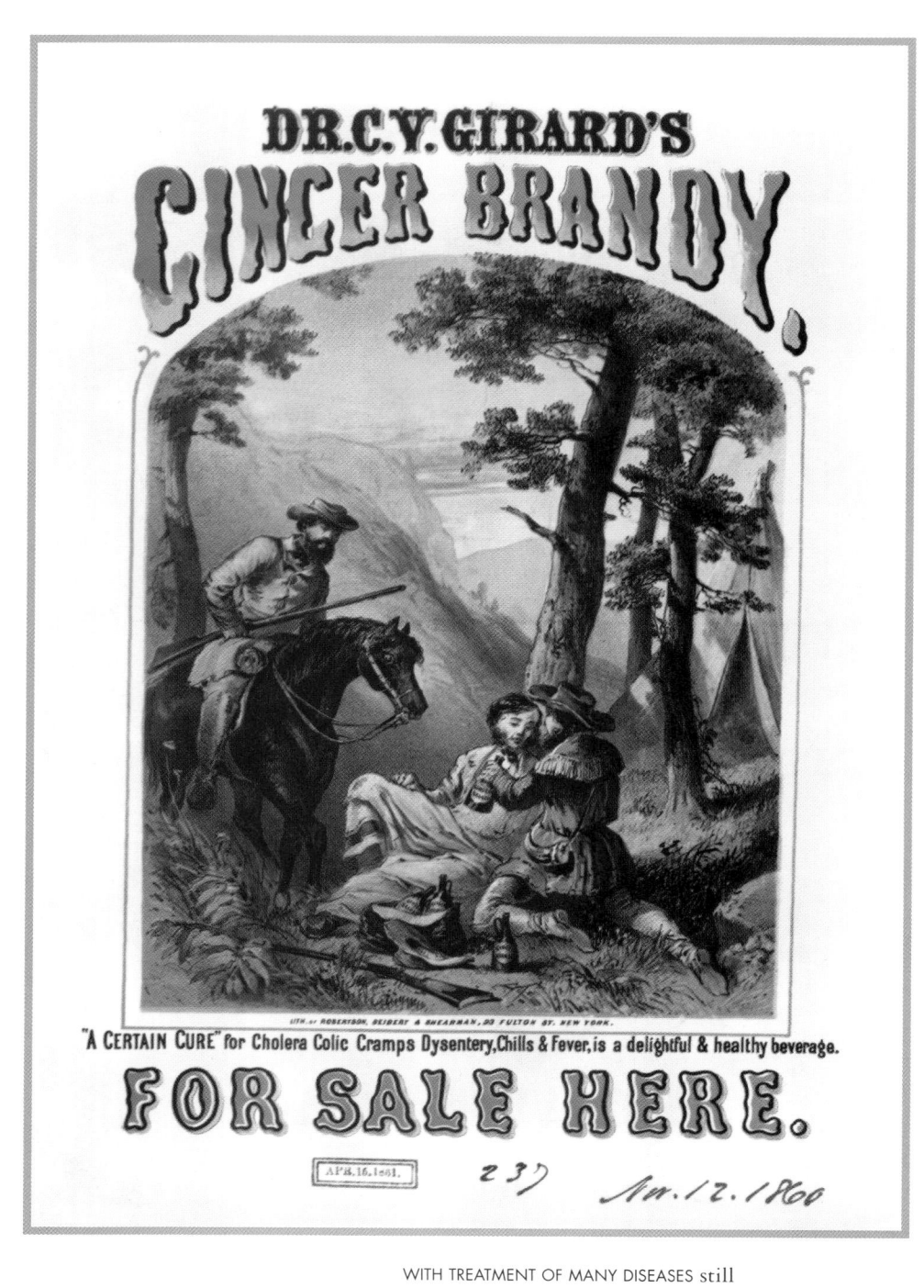

WITH TREATMENT OF MANY DISEASES still fairly hit-or-miss in the 19th century, and virtually no government authority empowered to regulate advertising claims, manufacturers of patent medicines were free to claim any curative powers they chose for their products. Consequently, "Dr. Girard's Ginger Brandy" declared itself "a certain cure" for cholera, as well as other ills, without fear of contradiction. Chances are, such miracles as it wrought were attributable to the temporary relief of strong liquors. Of similar efficacy was "Malt Bitters," which claimed to treat tuberculosis.

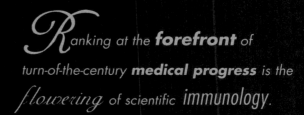

Chapter 4

*R*anking at the **forefront** of turn-of-the-century **medical progress** is the *flowering* of scientific immunology.

The Age *of* Biologics

1 8 9 4   t o   1 9 1 9

Despite periodic reforms directed at **cleaning up America's cities**, conditions in large urban areas remained notoriously poor at the end of the 19th century. A combination of swelling immigration and a spirit of social libertarianism made federal, state, and municipal regulation generally unwelcome and difficult to impose, except during epidemics and their attendant health emergencies. But sometime around 1890, a more progressive spirit entered public consciousness. With it, many of the nation's larger cities turned belatedly to comprehensive sanitation works. Piped and filtered water, underground sewer systems, systematic garbage collection, street cleaning, and sporadic school health programs contributed to the first significant improvements in average life expectancy in a century. By 1920, life expectancy in the United States had climbed dramatically to 57 years.

Somewhat slower to show any statistical effects on death and morbidity figures was a host of new medical interventions. Between 1880 and 1900 alone, distinct "germs" were identified as the causes of 21 specific diseases. As each became known, research was mounted to develop the appropriate "biologics," as this generation of vaccines was commonly termed. Year by year, the medical profession added to the strategies needed to ward off cholera, diphtheria, plague, pneumonia, tetanus, typhoid fever, and tuberculosis, as well as such common, but less lethal, contagious diseases as tularemia and hookworm.

Ranking at the forefront of turn-of-the-century medical progress, certainly, is the flowering of scientific immunology. Leading from Pasteur's work, his students Emile Roux and Alexandre Yersin found that in the cases of diphtheria and tetanus at least, it was not the bacteria that caused the deadly damage, but the resulting "toxins" (antigens) that were put into circulation in the blood. From there, Emil Von Behring, a Prussian army surgeon, and Shibasaburo Kitasato, a Japanese bacteriologist, teamed up to demonstrate that the body naturally reacts to such invasions by producing neutralizing "antitoxins" of its own. They went on to show that the antitoxins could be safely transferred from a formerly diseased body to a healthy one, producing "passive immunity" through an injection of blood serum. This discovery not only led almost immediately to effective treatments of tetanus and diphtheria, but opened the way to the analyses of the serum and cellular mechanisms—antibodies, phagocytes, lymphocytes, and so on—responsible for all immune responses.

Viruses, whose submicroscopic size and unorthodox behaviors had made them previously unknown and unknowable, were detected for the first time in 1898.

Another great advance in this era was the invention of the x-ray machine in 1895 by the Wurtzburg physicist Wilhelm Roentgen. Within two years of Roentgen's announcement, machines were beginning to be used in the offices of ordinary physicians, not just to see broken bones and wayward bullets, but to diagnose and monitor tuberculosis of the lungs.

Yellow fever was also contained. Though various theories of transmission had been proposed over the years, it was only when the United States began eyeing Panama as an imperial target that finding the causes and treatment of this complex tropical disease became a national priority. To tackle the problem, a military commission was sent to Cuba, where the United States had an occupation force following victory in the Spanish-American War. In 1901, Dr. Walter Reed, the commission's leader, announced that the *Stegomyia fasciata* mosquito was an intermediate host of the disease, transmitting infection from human to human via its bite. Another member of the commission, Dr. William Gorgas, a sanitary engineer with the Army, immediately set about to isolate every infected person on the island and to eradicate as nearly as possible the habitat for disease-bearing mosquitoes. The same empirical approach—a combination of better sanitation, vector control, and public education—was used to tackle yellow fever in the jungles of Panama and to thwart parasitic hookworm in the American South.

Viruses, whose submicroscopic size and unorthodox behaviors had made them previously unknown and unknowable, were detected for the first time in 1898. This set off a new round of investigations that would ultimately lead to understanding and treating a host of infectious diseases that had been presumed to have a bacterial cause.

Lastly, Germany's Paul Ehrlich became interested in what he perceived to be the "chemical affinity" of certain tissues in the body for particular chemical agents. Focusing on syphilis as a potentially appropriate disease state for his studies, and arsenical compounds, he found on his 606th trial a compound that bound uniquely to the bacteria responsible for the infection. Ehrlich's compound became the treatment of choice for syphilis up until relatively recent times and laid the foundations for the explosive growth of modern chemotherapy.

But as the era ended, the public and the medical profession received a sharp reminder that much more was needed to be learned about disease transmission if people were to feel safe from unprovoked attack. Between 1918 and 1919, at the end of World War I, a pandemic of influenza exploded. Unlike the more familiar visitations of influenza, which could cause high fevers, severe cold-like symptoms, and coughing in a community for a few weeks and then move on with relatively few consequences, the so-called "Spanish Flu" displayed a ferocity previously unknown. Substantial numbers of the infected succumbed within 48 hours to a fast-moving and deadly form of bacterial pneumonia. Though Congress called upon the new Public Health Service to turn all its attentions to containing the disease, only time brought the epidemic to an end. When it was over, flu had struck five million Americans, killing one in ten of them. With the world death toll estimated at 30 million, it was very possibly the single most severe contagion ever to invade the earth.

THE US ARMY MEDICAL DEPARTMENT found itself woefully understaffed and ill-prepared in handling casualties during the Spanish-American War. Especially difficult were the many cases of typhoid and yellow fever contracted in Cuba. Congress authorized the hiring of female nurses, and some 1600 were signed on beginning in May 1898. Many of the volunteers went to land-based hospitals, but the six intrepid women shown here were assigned to the USS Relief, a 750-bed floating hospital that sailed from Tampa to Cuba.

IN 1881, A CUBAN PHYSICIAN, Dr. Carlos Finlay, proposed that the source of yellow fever infection was the common house mosquito, but lacking experimental evidence, his theory was largely ignored. In the meantime, concern over the spread of disease from one infected patient to another prompted the use of portable isolation cages, like the one shown above.

IN JUNE 1900, Dr. Walter Reed was sent
to Cuba at the head of the Yellow Fever
Commission; its mission was to test Carlos
Finlay's theory. During this effort, two
commission members contracted yellow
fever, one of them dying, but they did
prove Finlay correct. To combat the disease,
Reed ordered a mosquito eradication
campaign led by sanitation expert Major
William Gorgas, and within a year Havana
had been made safe from the deadly disease.

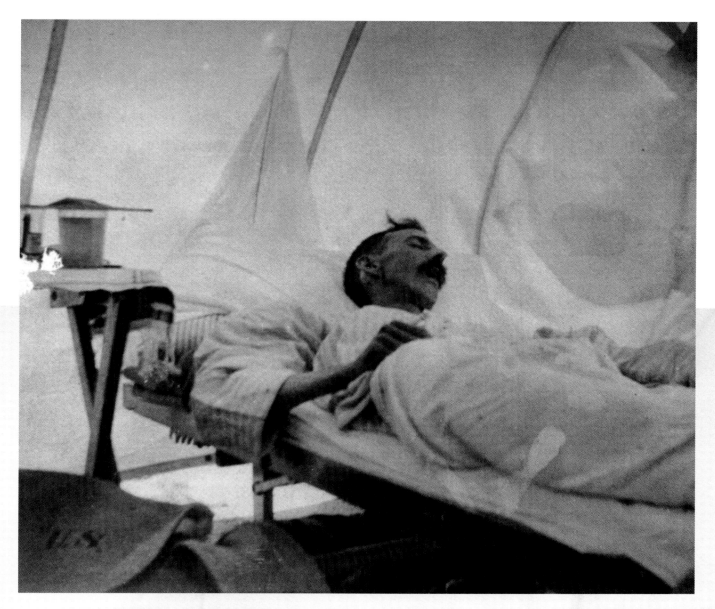

YELLOW FEVER TYPICALLY OVERTOOK ITS VICTIMS within four or five days of becoming infected, expressing itself through fever, jaundice, hemorrhaging in the stomach and intestinal tract, and "black vomit." Mortality rates for individuals like the very sick soldier shown here in a field hospital ran as high as 70%.

BUBONIC PLAGUE APPEARED FOR THE FIRST TIME in North America on March 6, 1900, when a Chinese shopkeeper was found dead in the basement of a shabby hotel in San Francisco. For more than a year, local authorities chose to deny its existence, fearing bad publicity. But when many more cases surfaced, the US Public Health Service was called in. They sent a large team of workers to set up a semipermanent branch office in the city. One of their chief methods of control was through a rigorous sanitation drive in the 12 square blocks of Chinatown, where nearly 14 000 rooms were scrubbed with a mercury solution and household goods were fumigated.

EVENTUALLY, AFTER EIGHT YEARS OF VIGOROUS RODENT CONTROL, San Francisco's plague was effectively eradicated. To monitor the Service's progress, officers routinely scoured the Bay area for squirrels and rats, dissecting thousands of them for telltale signs of the disease. Shown here is a field team c.1905. Plague subsequently appeared in New Orleans, where the Public Health Service was called in to take charge of plague control operations. Trapping and inspecting rats—up to 5000 per day—continued to be a central part of the effort.

IN THE 1890s, doctors embraced the rest cure and fresh air as the best recourse for tuberculosis care, and sanitariums specifically devoted to the care of "consumptives" were opened near every metropolitan center. The most famous of the early establishments was the Adirondack Cottage facility founded in 1884 by Dr. Edward Trudeau, himself a former patient, at pristine Saranac Lake in New York's Adirondack Mountains. Trudeau experimented with a variety of therapies, including inhalation therapy that delivered carbolic acid–laden air to patients encased in breathing cabinets. But his greatest enthusiasm lay in fresh air treatments, the more the better, in all seasons and temperatures. In wintertime, ambulatory patients were encouraged to bundle up and spend their days snowshoeing around the sanitarium's large campus, as recorded in this 1894 snapshot (below). Those who were capable only of sitting were given special reclining "cure chairs" and directed to sit out on one of the many deep verandas where they might quietly socialize while recuperating (right).

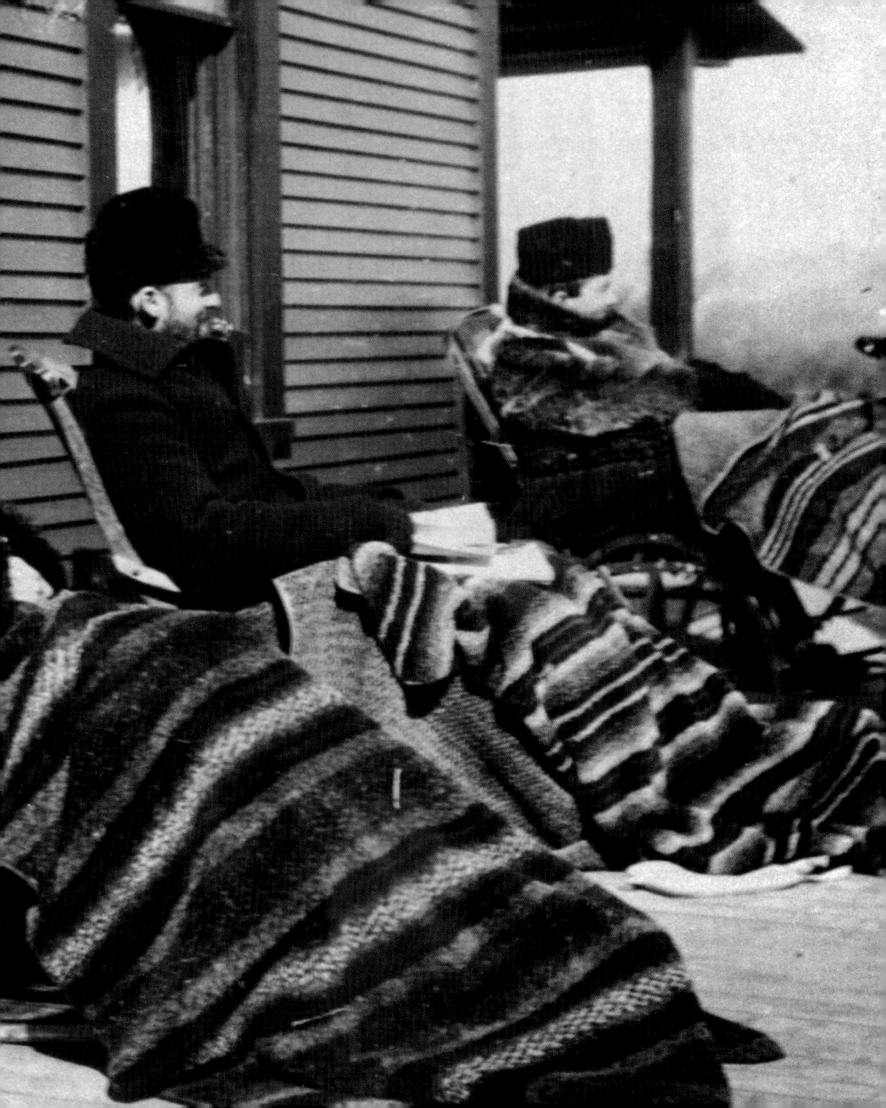

DESPITE KOCH'S LANDMARK ACHIEVEMENT in isolating the tubercle bacillus in 1882, the disease still ranked as the primary cause of death in the United States in 1900. In the 1908 photo above, a victim of tuberculosis is being loaded into a horse-drawn vehicle for transport to a St. Paul, Minnesota, hospital. The same fine carriage was also available as a hearse, should treatment not prove successful.

IT WAS COMMONLY BELIEVED that tuberculosis, as well as many other communicable diseases, was the handmaiden of poor housekeeping. Charitable organizations in some cities consequently sought ways to instruct the "unwashed" in developing better habits. To penetrate households of poor Italian immigrants, New York's Community Service Society launched a novel poster campaign in 1908. The society had printed a colorful illustration of a canal in Venice, together with some educational information on tuberculosis. A young Italian woman who had recovered from the disease was hired to go door-to-door with her complimentary art offering, and in short order she reportedly talked with some 2000 families living in Manhattan's crowded Lower East Side tenements. The Society had similar programs to reach other large ethnic groups.

LEPROSY, A DISEASE WELL KNOWN SINCE ANCIENT TIMES, was first recognized in this country in the late 19th century when Louisiana quietly opened its own leprosarium in Carville, at a bend in the Mississippi River. So much fear was attached to the disease that the director of the hospital initially claimed to be running an ostrich farm there. Early treatment included the application of traditional remedies including chaulmoogra oil, an antibacterial chemical rendered from the seeds of the Asian chaulmoogra tree. The Carville facility, which since 1917 has been managed by the US Public Health Service, continues to house and treat patients, whose numbers nationwide total an estimated 6000. Today, dapsone, a sulfa drug, is the primary medication for controlling leprosy.

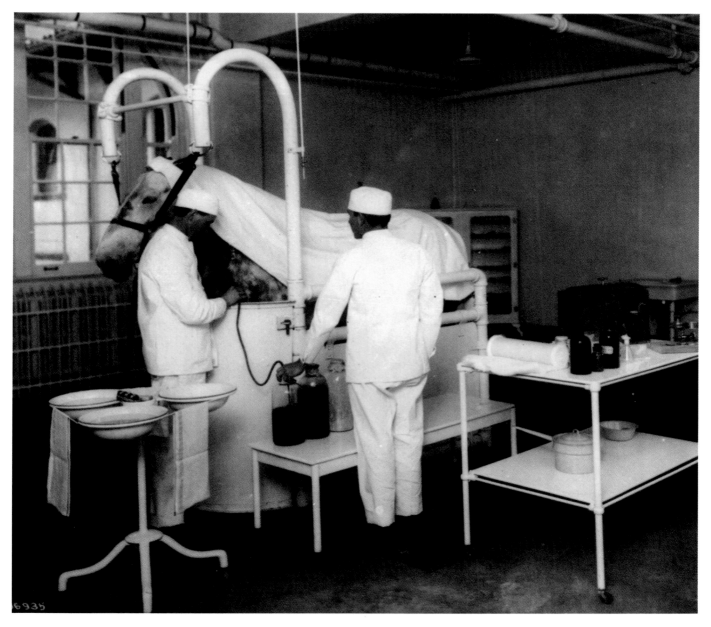

ONCE ROUX AND YERSIN showed that the disease of diphtheria was produced by a bacterial poison, or toxin, it
was a relatively simple matter to develop serum therapy
and prophylaxis against the disease. Diphtheria antitoxins were first tested on humans in Berlin in 1891
and were widely available after 1894. In this 1910
photograph, taken in one of the pharmaceutical laboratories at Eli Lilly, Indianapolis, Indiana, a horse previously infected with human diphtheria has some of its
blood withdrawn. The blood, rich in antibodies, was
processed subsequently and the relevant antitoxins used
to prepare human diphtheria vaccine. Three years after
this photo was taken, the Hungarian bacteriologist
Bela Schick developed the universal test for diphtheria
immunity that bears his name.

TULAREMIA, AN INFECTIOUS DISEASE CHIEFLY OF RODENTS, has been described as "the first American disease." It was first noted and studied in the human population, most of them small game hunters, in the American West. As squirrels and rabbits were found to be the primary carriers of the disease, massive eradication drives were organized by the Public Health Service early in this century. US Public Health Service investigators isolated the pathogenic bacteria, *Pasteurella tularensis*, in 1912. Another scientist, Edward Francis, demonstrated its presence in man in 1919, naming the disease after Tulare County, California, where it was first discovered. Francis is shown here as he inoculates a rabbit with "rabbit fever."

1. GARDNER
2. AMESSE
3. WHITE
4. Gov BLANCHARD
5. BLUE
6. McMULLEN
7. CURRIE
8. McKEON
9. ASHFORD
10. DE VALIN

11. BERRY
12. RICHARDSE
13. GOLDBERGE
14. CORPUT
15. EBERT
16. RUCKER
17. STEGER
18. GUTHRIE
19. FROST

POSING FOR A FORMAL GROUP PORTRAIT, 18 commissioned and uniformed officers of the Public Health and Marine Hospital Service pose with Governor Blanchard of Louisiana. By this time, the Public Health Service was fully engaged in protecting aspects of civilian health. In this particular instance, they were serving in the campaign against yellow fever in New Orleans in 1905.

EVER SINCE THE END OF THE CIVIL WAR, the North had tended to look down on the rural South, whose farmers were notably less productive than those in other parts of the country. Many dismissed Southerners' slowness as pure laziness, but investigations by Charles Wardell Stiles, a young officer in the Public Health Service's new Division of Zoology, suggested that a blood-sucking intestinal parasite, which he called hookworm, was at work. Realizing that the funds and manpower needed to fight the disease far exceeded the Service's budget, Stiles enlisted the patronage of John D. Rockefeller. In 1908 the philanthropist endowed the new Rockefeller Sanitary Commission with $1 million to be spent over the next five years in the 13 Southern states. Stiles' campaign focused on changes in privy construction and in behavior, especially the wearing of shoes. Hookworm typically infects individuals through cuts and wounds in bare feet.

AT ONE OF THE HUNDREDS OF DISPENSARIES OPENED by the Rockefeller Sanitary
Commission, citizens of Lincoln County, North Carolina, are offered a demonstration
and free medicine. The cure, costing a mere 50 cents per person, consisted of a dose
of thymol followed by a chaser of Epsom salts, sufficient to dislodge and expel the
parasites. The men sitting at the tables are Commission workers who use their
microscopes to demonstrate the presence of hookworm in the human waste that
was often casually disposed of in substandard privies.

THE ROCKEFELLER SANITARY COMMISSION was also interested in the location of public wells and the purity of their water. The example above, located at the bottom of a hill where seven privies drained, was a case in point. The Commissioners noted, too, that the well had no bucket of its own. Users lowered whatever container they brought into the well, thereby adding another source of contamination.

FIELD WORKERS CAME TO RECOGNIZE the telltale appearance of hookworm anemia, which one described as "a striking lankiness of frame, slackness of muscle, shambling gait, boniness and misshapen head and features, sallow swarthiness." The photo above shows the effects of hookworm on three generations of a Hawkins County, Tennessee, family. In the photo (left), a young man from Cerro Gordo, North Carolina, stands firm seven weeks after treatment, his hemoglobin having risen from 14% to 55% and his red blood cell count having more than quadrupled.

IN 1911 DR. LESLIE LUMSDEN, a Public Health Service doctor with a distinguished record in typhoid fever research, was sent to Yakima County in the State of Washington to investigate the source of a particularly virulent outbreak. His conclusion was that the cause lay in the poor levels of waste sanitation, and he launched a drive to replace existing privies with improved models. Lumsden's published research became a blueprint for the work of the newly emerging county health departments around the country. One method of control was to make waste disposal a municipal service. Carts like the one shown at work in Mitchell, Indiana, became a familiar sight, with one of "Lumsden's boys" picking up full waste cans and delivering fresh ones on a regular schedule.

SANITARY REFORM was something that needed
the backing of all parts of the community.
Here, a local pharmacy pitches in with a
prominent window display of a novel
product called "toilet paper" and some
brochures on privy maintenance.

AS KNOWLEDGE OF DISEASE CONTROL INCREASED, efforts at prevention grew exponentially. In this photograph taken in the rural South in the early years of the 20th century, Public Health Service officers accompanied by the local preacher stop at a school yard to inoculate boys against typhoid. The program was a bonus offering associated with a more ambitious campaign to raise sanitary levels.

CHILDREN HAVE ALWAYS SUFFERED a disproportionate share of infectious diseases, owing to their immature immune systems and the fact that exposure is a prerequisite to developing acquired immunity. Before antibiotics, middle-ear infections had the potential to develop into mastoiditis followed by deadly meningitis. A surgical procedure, involving an incision behind the ear and the removal of the diseased mastoid bone, was developed late in the 18th century and remained the treatment of choice. Here, a row of postsurgical patients are recovering at Cook County Contagion Hospital, Chicago, in 1912. Children also were prime victims of a host of serious respiratory infections, including pneumonia and tuberculosis. For a group of convalescing patients at Boston's Children's Hospital in 1905, the prescribed treatment was a daily dose of rest time in the "pure, fresh air" of a so-called "Wellesley shack."

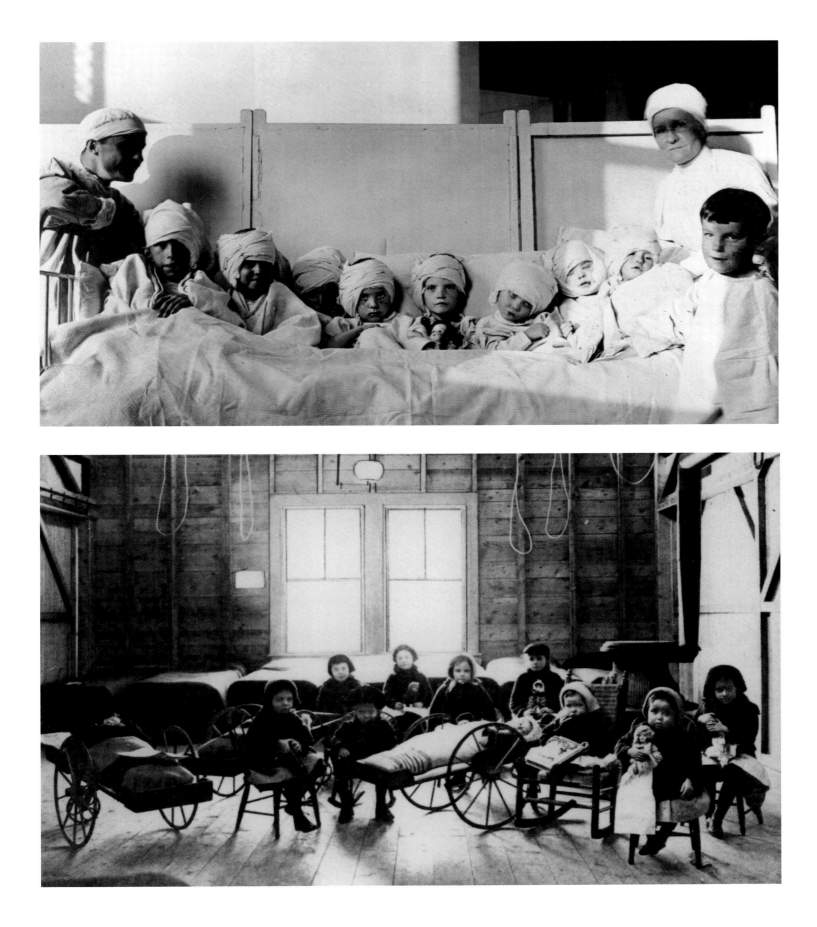

THE EXISTENCE OF VIRUSES as agents of disease
was first hinted at in 1892, but it was not
until the electron microscope was developed
in the 1930s that these infinitesimally
small agents could be seen. Nonetheless,
Peyton Rous of the Rockefeller Institute
was able to deduce by a series of experiments with tumor-bearing chickens that
among lower animals, at least, certain can-
cers could be generated by an infectious
agent. Rous went on to determine that
the agent was something smaller and more
elusive than bacteria, for it passed through
the finest of bacterial filters. Rous' theories
were later proved correct, and the search
began for human carcinogenic viruses.

IN ORDER TO ISOLATE AND STUDY disease-causing microorganisms under the microscope, late 19th-century researchers had used various staining agents. In this way, the German bacteriologist Paul Ehrlich discovered that a certain red dye not only selected out the trypanosome organism responsible for sleeping sickness, but killed it. Ehrlich and his Japanese assistant Sahachiro Hata went on to study arsenical variations on the so-called trypan red, hoping to find other chemical bacteriacides. In 1909, they found that compound 606, later given the name of Salvarsan, was a highly effective treatment for syphilis. Ehrlich called his compound a "magic bullet" because it killed the harmful pathogens with relatively few side effects to the patient.

BATTLEFIELD INFECTIONS were a constant and urgent concern. Here, soldiers of the 82nd and 89th divisions of the American Expeditionary Force, victims of a mustard gas attack, lie on newly plowed farm fields awaiting evacuation to a hospital near Royaumeix, France. As the fields were routinely fertilized with animal and human excrement, the opportunity for bacteria, especially tetanus bacilli, to contaminate cuts and wounds was great. At the outbreak of war, the incidence of tetanus ran at an extraordinarily high 8 per 1000 with an 80% mortality. But before it ended, an antitoxin against tetanus came into wide use, the result of work begun by Koch and Kitasato nearly a quarter century earlier. Incidence of tetanus among the Allied forces fell to just 0.6 per 1000.

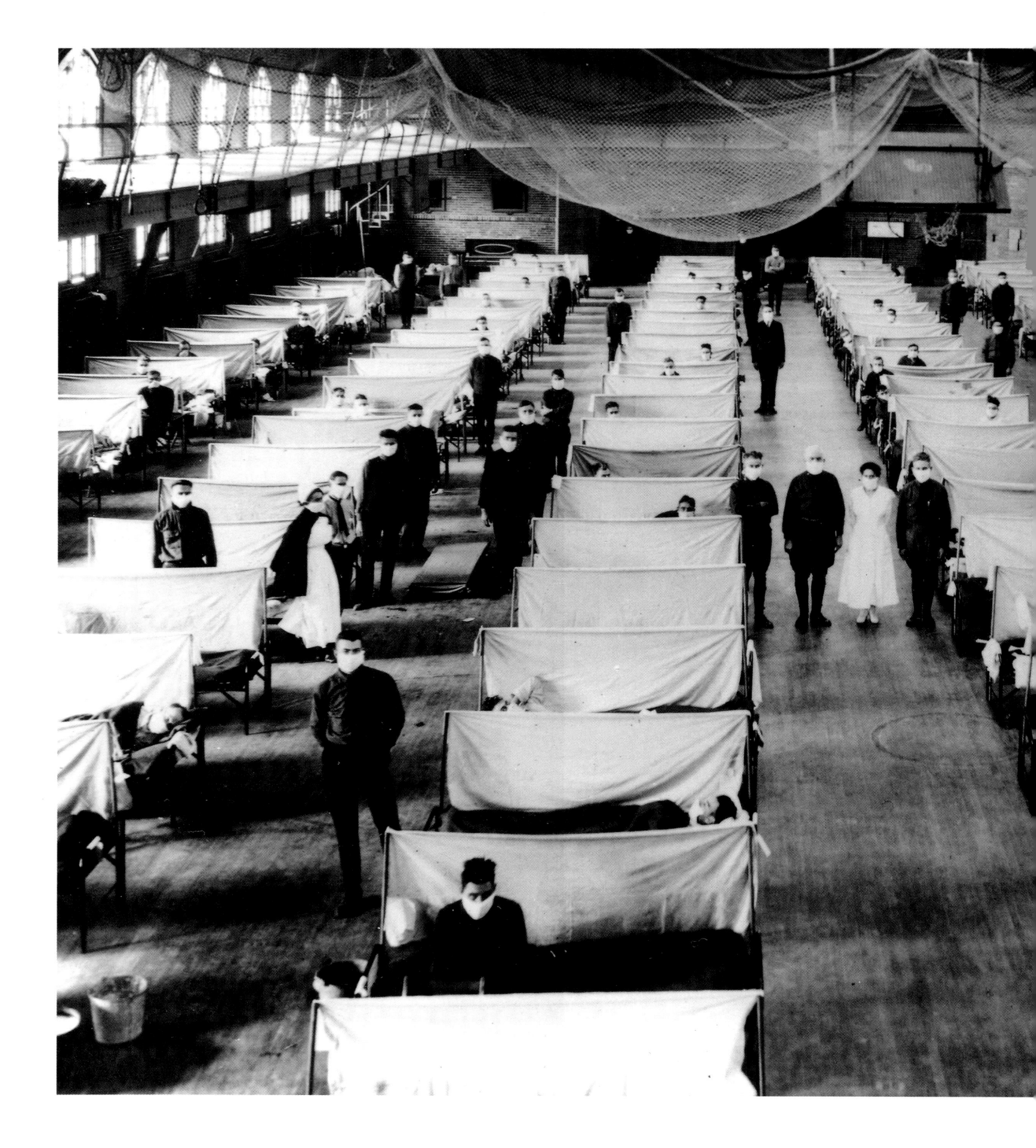

LATE IN AUGUST 1918, a particularly deadly strain of the influenza virus entered Boston, one of the ports actively engaged in the transport of men to the European war zone. Variously known as "La Grippe" and the "Spanish Flu," this flu had an alarming tendency to give way to pneumonia. Victims often turned "blue as huckleberries," according to one physician, and died in a day or two. Remarkably, it was young people in the prime of life who suffered the highest rates of mortality. To meet the national emergency, Congress voted the Public Health Service a $1 million appropriation to hire additional doctors and nurses to care for the sick. Massive infirmaries like the one in a gymnasium at the Iowa State University in Ames were opened across the country. But there was little that medicine could do for the sufferers but offer comfort and urge the public to stay home and away from contact with others, as the precautionary poster posted in Chicago indicates. Altogether, the United States suffered almost 650 000 deaths, about one person in every 150.

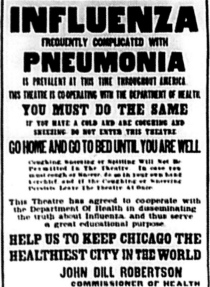

Chapter 5

In nature microorganisms often compete with one another, the **stronger ones** eventually defeating the *weaker* in a kind of **Darwinian** struggle.

The Age
of Antibiotics

1 9 2 0   t o   1 9 4 8

As early as the mid-19th century, **serious students** of the biological sciences had recognized that in nature microorganisms often compete with one another, the stronger ones eventually defeating the weaker in a kind of Darwinian struggle. This process, which one early bacteriologist called "antibiosis," hinted at the possibility that specific diseases could be inhibited or destroyed through matching them with the right antagonists. But finding safe and effective combinations required close cooperation between chemists and biologists and a more advanced pharmaceutical industry than existed. Still, hundreds of experiments were tried on a hit-and-miss basis, and finally beginning in the late 1920s, scientists in England and Germany made the first discoveries that would lead directly to the introduction of natural antibiotics and their subsequent nonorganic cousins, the antibacterials. Capable of controlling a wide range of bacterial infections in ways scarcely imagined earlier, these discoveries would become the "wonder drugs" of the modern era. Credit for the first major discovery—penicillin—is generally given to the Scottish bacteriologist Sir Alexander Fleming. Working one day in 1928 in his "germ laboratory" at London's St. Mary's Hospital, Fleming noticed that a culture of staphylococcus bacteria that he had been developing had accidentally become contaminated with airborne spores of *Penicillium* mold. To the researcher's even greater surprise, wherever the mold colony and the bacteria were touching, the bacteria was inexorably dying. Fleming went on to study the action of the uninvited fungus and found that it was selective in its action, inhibiting or even killing some species of bacteria, but having no effect on others. He also found it to have no negative effect on either laboratory animals or on the white cells of human blood. Fleming's low-key report of his findings in a British medical journal eventually caught the attention of other researchers, and as penicillin's disease-fighting potential became increasingly clear over the next few years, excitement grew. The problem was how to brew it in volume. Finally, under the pressure of wartime emergency, scientists at a US Department of Agriculture laboratory in Peoria, Illinois, solved this final hurdle in 1943. By 1944, the US drug industry was working in collaboration to produce nearly 1600 billion units of penicillin under contract to the War Department, thus saving tens of thousands of lives from battlefield infections.

Sulfa drugs, which reached full-scale production even before the war, were first discovered in 1932 by Gerhard Domagk, a Polish-born German biologist. Experimenting with the antimicrobial potential of textile dyes, Domagk found that a red textile dye, Prontosil, had a high potential for killing streptococcal bacteria and reversing blood poisoning in mice. In the next few years, researchers went on to isolate the active ingredient sulfanilamide in Prontosil, and drug companies rushed to find their own proprietary version of the antibacterial drug. By 1941, there were numerous sulfa drugs on the market, with 1700 tons of the sulfur and nitrogen compound reportedly reaching the market in a single year. Various sulfonamides were quickly adopted as the treatment of choice for several kinds of pneumonias, blood poisoning, erysipelas, mastoiditis, rheumatic fever, bacterial endocarditis, urinary tract infections, and trachoma. Packets of sulfanilamides were also included in the first-aid kit of every combat soldier. Not until other antibacterials proved more appropriate for many conditions did the wholesale use of sulfa drugs decrease to their current, more limited use primarily in treating urinary tract infections.

Good for infections ranging from bronchitis and venereal diseases to cholera and Rocky Mountain spotted fever, the tetracyclines have proved particularly important as many infections have become resistant in the intervening years to penicillin.

Two other important antibiotics to be discovered in this period are streptomycin and aureomycin. True antibiotics, both were initially developed from soil-dwelling bacteria. Streptomycin was identified in 1939 by Selman Waksman of Rutgers University. Waksman systematically tested some 10 000 soil samples before finding one effective against some kinds of tuberculosis. Although other antibiotics have since replaced streptomycin in all but a few resistant strains of tuberculosis, Waksman's discovery remains a reliable agent in treating a number of other uncommon infections. Aureomycin, the first in a collection of tetracyclines, came along at the end of the war, adding yet another broad-spectrum contender in the new armamentarium against infectious diseases. Good for infections ranging from bronchitis and venereal diseases to cholera and Rocky Mountain spotted fever, the tetracyclines have proved particularly important as many infections have become resistant in the intervening years to penicillin.

Wonderful as the new antibiotics proved to be, they were irrelevant to viral infections, whose unique mechanisms were only beginning to be imagined, much less understood, in the early decades of the century. But beginning in the 1930s, even the mysteries of viruses were yielding to modern research. Advances in technology, including development of the electron microscope and high-speed centrifuges, made it possible to examine and study these once-invisible particles close up. New methods of reproducing the viruses in chicken embryos also enhanced discovery. And although no one was as yet able to find a "magic bullet" equivalent to antibiotics for any of the viruses, work on viral vaccines continued to bear fruit. In 1933 researchers established that influenza was not a bacterial infection after all, but a complex group of viral infections, and this led to the development of the first flu vaccine in 1945. The first effective yellow fever and typhus vaccines were also readied, and work on poliomyelitis got under way in earnest.

Meanwhile, the trend toward government involvement in protecting the public health accelerated under Roosevelt's New Deal programs. Beginning in the 1930s, federal monies were invested in vaccine development, in educational initiatives against venereal disease, in rural malaria control, and in the creation of the National Institutes of Health and the Centers for Disease Control, to list just the most prominent efforts. The public health programs turned out to be good practice for America's wartime mobilization. They also proved valuable rehearsals for later efforts, albeit under United Nations' sponsorship, to confront the growing internationalization of health and disease issues.

THE WISCONSIN ANTI-TUBERCULOSIS ASSOCIATION reached out to citizens via a traveling health clinic that offered low-cost chest x-rays and educational materials. As shown in this c.1935 photo, public concern remained high. According to the display, there were an estimated 10 000 cases of tuberculosis currently in Wisconsin, "many of them still unknown." Death from the disease was always a possibility; in the previous year, 1048 Wisconsinites had reportedly died of tuberculosis-related causes.

THE 1920S SAW AN INCREASE in publicity and fund-raising events for all manner of health causes. This tableau vivant, launching a Christmas Health Stamp sale, was staged in Minneapolis, Minnesota, in 1924. It benefited the National Tuberculosis Foundation, forerunner of the American Lung Association, an association of concerned physicians and other health professionals.

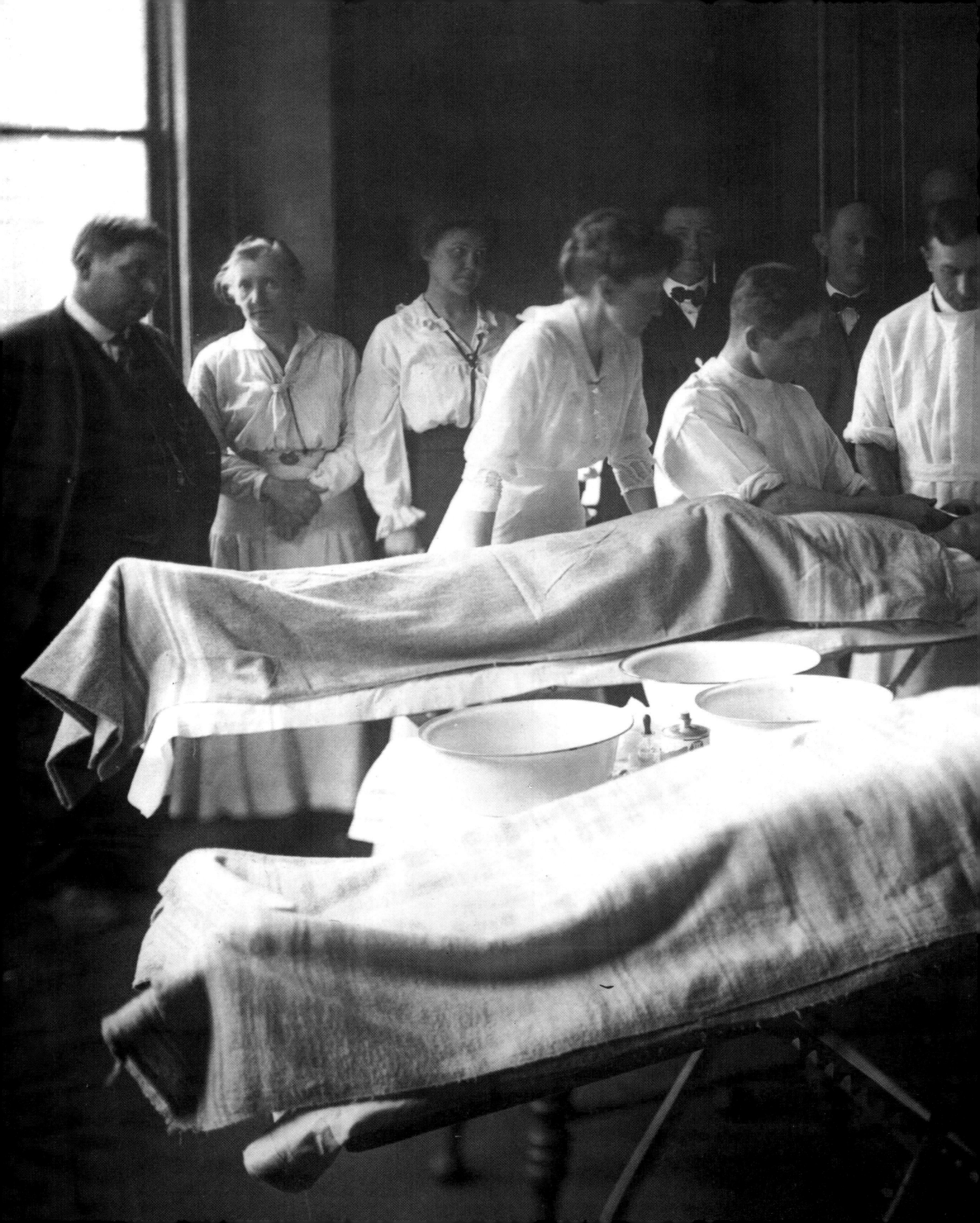

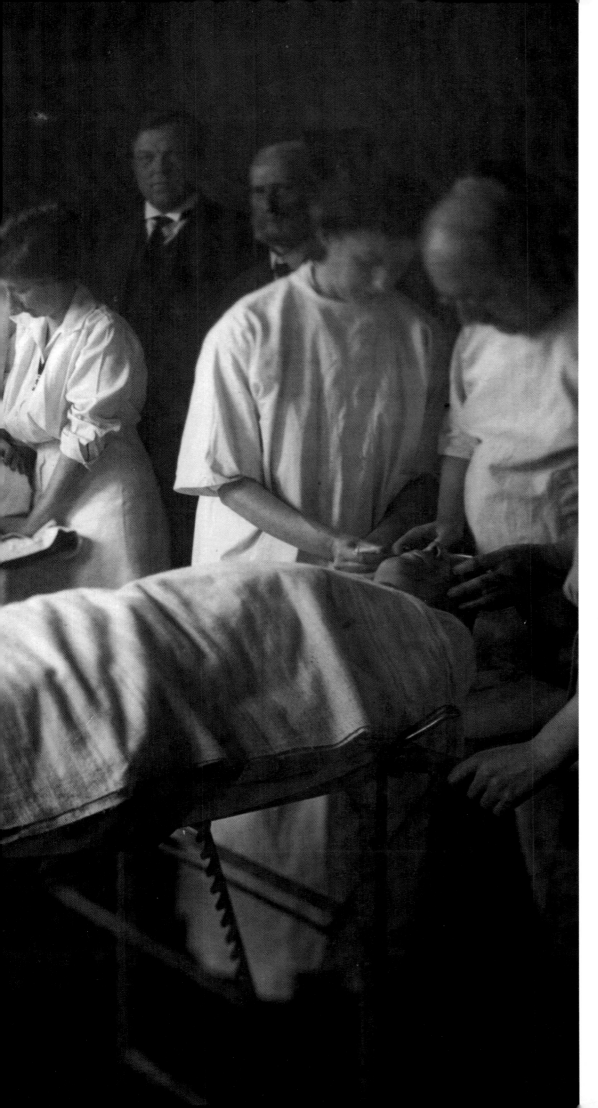

TRACHOMA, A HIGHLY INFECTIOUS DISEASE of the conjunctiva and cornea leading to blindness, flourished among the mountain people of the Appalachian South in the early years of the 20th century. With a federal appropriation voted in 1913, the Public Health Service launched a 15-year campaign to bring it under control. They set up more than a dozen temporary trachoma hospitals and scores of outlying clinics from West Virginia to Missouri, and sent in teams of doctors and nurses to treat patients and educate the well public regarding prevention. In the photo, two severely infected patients undergo surgical debridement of the eyelids to remove fibrous scar tissue. Less severe cases were treated with caustics such as silver nitrate. Sincere as these efforts were, cures were rare until the introduction of sulfonamide therapy in 1938.

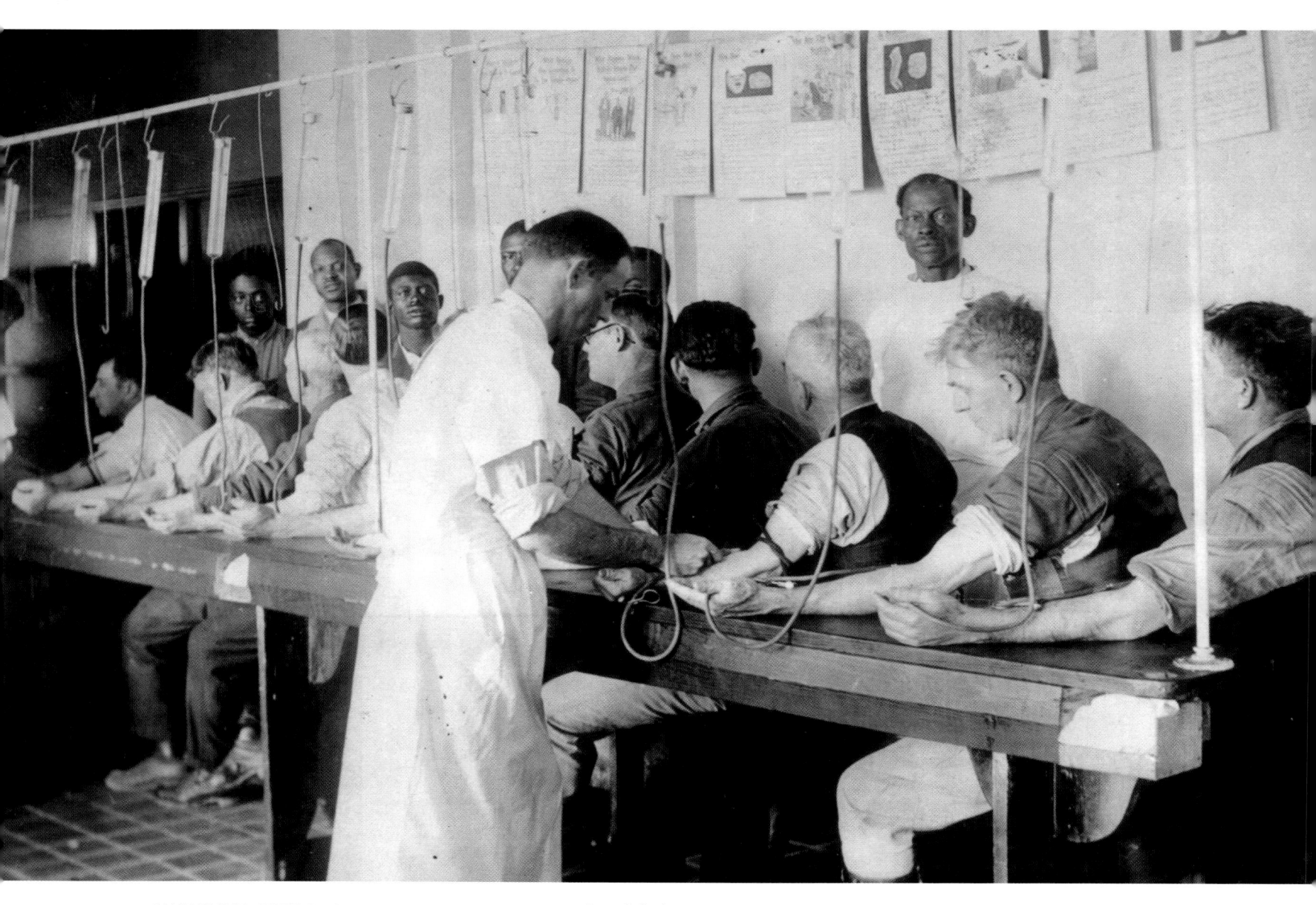

CAMPAIGNS TO CURTAIL THE SPREAD OF VENEREAL DISEASE were activated during
World War I and, despite a sharp decline in Congressional support after
war's end, the Public Health Service and many local agencies continued
the work in the decades following. Shown above is one of the research
and education clinics run at the Government Free Bath House in
Hot Springs, Arkansas. Another study of syphilis was undertaken at
Tuskegee, Alabama, in 1932. The infamous Tuskegee Project involved
400 African-American men known to have syphilis. The subjects were
recruited from churches and clinics throughout the South, where the rate
of disease among African-Americans was as high as 36% in some counties.
But unbeknownst to them, placebos rather than the standard treatments
of mercury and arsenic compounds were used, so as to observe the natural
course of syphilis. Still later, when the discovery of penicillin made
the complete cure of syphilis relatively certain, the participants in the
Tuskegee study continued to go without proper treatment. Only in 1972
were the deception and government culpability revealed and an out-of-
court settlement of money damages rendered the survivors.

ROCKY MOUNTAIN SPOTTED FEVER, or "black measles" as it was popularly known, was first isolated in Montana's Bitterroot Valley in the early years of the 20th century. A team sent out by the Public Health Service eventually identified the disease transmitted by the wood tick, and in 1917 a vaccine was developed. But it was not until the era of the New Deal that a major effort was launched to vaccinate the most susceptible members of the population. Shown above is one of the service's bacteriologists at work on Rocky Mountain spotted fever research. She prepares tissue cultures at the Washington, DC, Hygienic Laboratory, where since 1891 the Public Health Service had maintained its principal laboratory and research center.

ONCE THE PUBLIC HEALTH SERVICE'S **vaccination** drive for Rocky Mountain spotted fever got under way, officers were tireless in their pursuit of subjects. Here, a rancher is interrupted in his labors by a pair of far-ranging field agents.

MALARIA, WHICH WAS A PERSISTENT PUBLIC HEALTH CONCERN particularly in rural parts of the South, became the focus of a vigorous control program during the Depression. As mosquitos were the known vector, the spraying of breeding grounds was the most efficient means of attacking malaria. Here, federal workers use the then-popular insecticide "Paris green-lime," or copper acetoarsenite, to spray empty garbage cans in a back alley.

EPIDEMIOLOGY IS THE MEDICAL SCIENCE concerned with tracking the relationship of various factors and conditions that contribute to disease and its frequency. Researchers use the information collected and interpreted by epidemiologists to shape their clinical studies and assess the success or failure of various health initiatives. Before the era of computers, the collection of the vast amounts of statistical information needed was a slow and painstaking process, as these workers in the Public Health Service's Statistical Office demonstrate.

CONCERTED INTEREST IN A CAMPAIGN against polio developed in 1921 when Franklin D. Roosevelt, an emerging figure in national politics, came down with paralytic poliomyelitis. Scion of a wealthy family, Roosevelt invested the better part of his personal fortune to establish the Georgia Warm Springs Foundation as a center for the care and rehabilitation of patients like himself. Following Roosevelt's election as President of the United States, he used his prestige to launch the National Foundation for Infantile Paralysis and its fund-raising arm, the March of Dimes. Above, Roosevelt is seen with two of the many youngsters who were treated at Warm Springs. Right, children, many of them in wheelchairs, gather in the Warm Springs auditorium for some entertainment.

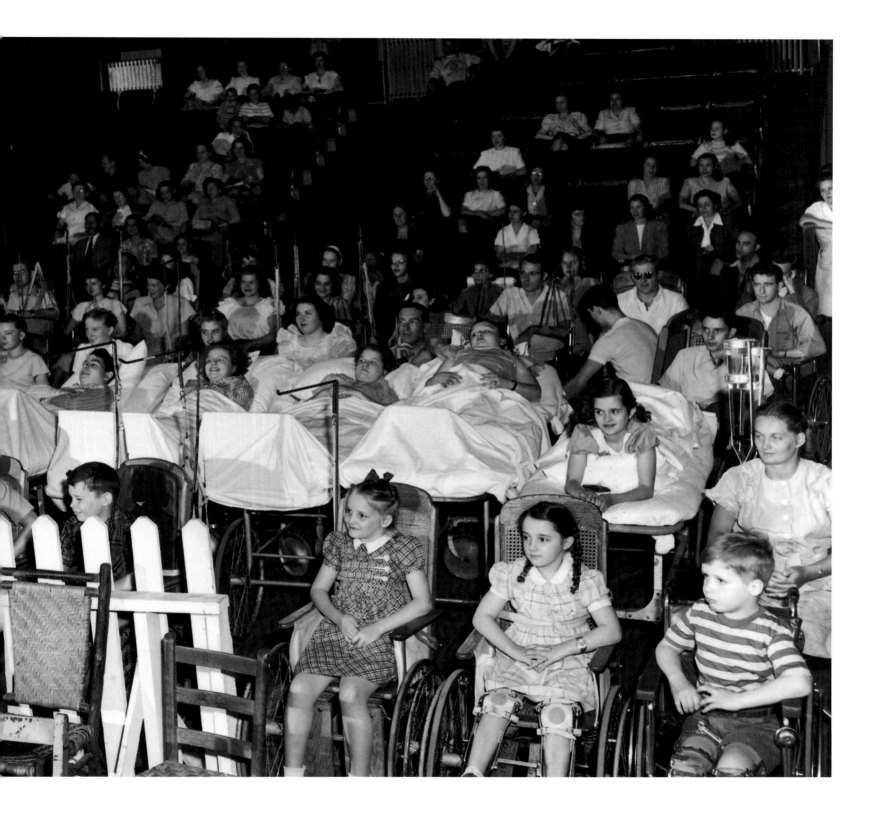

MEDICAL SCIENTISTS HAD KNOWN SINCE 1909 that polio was a viral disease, but little else about its transmission or control had been learned since. As the incidence of persons infected grew, ordinary folks took whatever defensive measures they could imagine. Here, at an urban dump site in Philadelphia in 1932, an official sets fire to a pile of old mattresses in the mistaken belief that they may contain polio "germs."

SOON AFTER FRENCHMAN PAUL VUILLEMIN described the condition in nature when "one creature destroys the life of another to preserve its own" in 1889, researchers began searching in earnest for antagonistic bacterial agents known as "antibiotes." Literally hundreds of research papers reporting on such actions followed, but it was not until 1928 that the era of modern antibiotic medicine can be said to have begun. In that year, a Scottish bacteriologist named Sir Alexander Fleming chanced to discover the potent inhibitory effects of a certain *Penicillium* mold, especially in combating such Gram-positive bacteria as staphylococci, streptococci, and pneumococci. Fleming, shown in his laboratory above, left the development of a viable form of penicillin to two scientific heirs at Oxford University, Howard Florey and Ernst Chain. The first doses of the antibiotic were ready for trial in 1941.

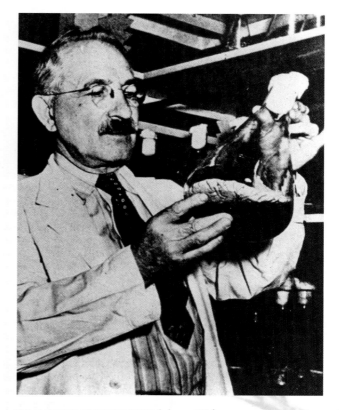

THE AMERICAN MICROBIOLOGIST Selman Waksman developed another major antibiotic, streptomycin, in 1944. Recognized almost immediately as an effective treatment for two of the principal types of tuberculosis, streptomycin was subsequently found to be antagonistic to the bacteria underlying such now rare diseases as tularemia, plague, brucellosis, and glanders.

SINCE THE FIRST DECADE OF THE 20TH CENTURY, both the bacteria causing syphilis and the Wassermann Test for detecting their presence were widely known in the medical community. And thanks to Paul Ehrlich's Salvarsan, there was medication to treat it. Nonetheless, the sexually transmitted disease remained a difficult problem socially and medically. In the years just before World War II, the Public Health Service received major government funding to create a separate Venereal Disease Division and engage the disease with research and educational programs. This pre-war street demonstration was held in Chicago with Public Health Service support.

AFTER WAR WAS DECLARED, programs aimed specifically at the armed forces were added to the Public Health Service's list of responsibilities. Posters like the one above were widely displayed, cautionary films were shown as part of basic training, and condoms were made available for the asking. In recognition that prostitutes would inevitably encamp close by military bases, the service also ran convenient clinics to treat women who were infected.

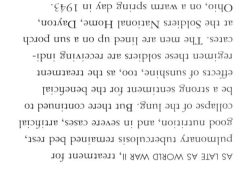

AS LATE AS WORLD WAR II, treatment for pulmonary tuberculosis remained bed rest, good nutrition, and in severe cases, artificial collapse of the lung. But there continued to be a strong sentiment for the beneficial effects of sunshine, too, as the treatment regimen these soldiers are receiving indicates. The men are lined up on a sun porch at the Soldiers National Home, Dayton, Ohio, on a warm spring day in 1943.

THE WORLD-FAMOUS CENTERS for Disease Control and Prevention got its start in 1942 as the Atlanta, Georgia–based operation known as Malaria Control in War Areas, or MCWA. The campaign began with draining swamps and spreading larvicides. Its responsibilities grew in scope as typhus control was added and preparations launched to screen returning servicemen for what medical experts anticipated would be a spate of unfamiliar tropical diseases from the South Pacific. Here, workers of the MCWA work through the night on a typhus control assignment, building rat traps. Colleagues in the field also dusted rat runs with DDT, whose value as an insecticide had just been discovered.

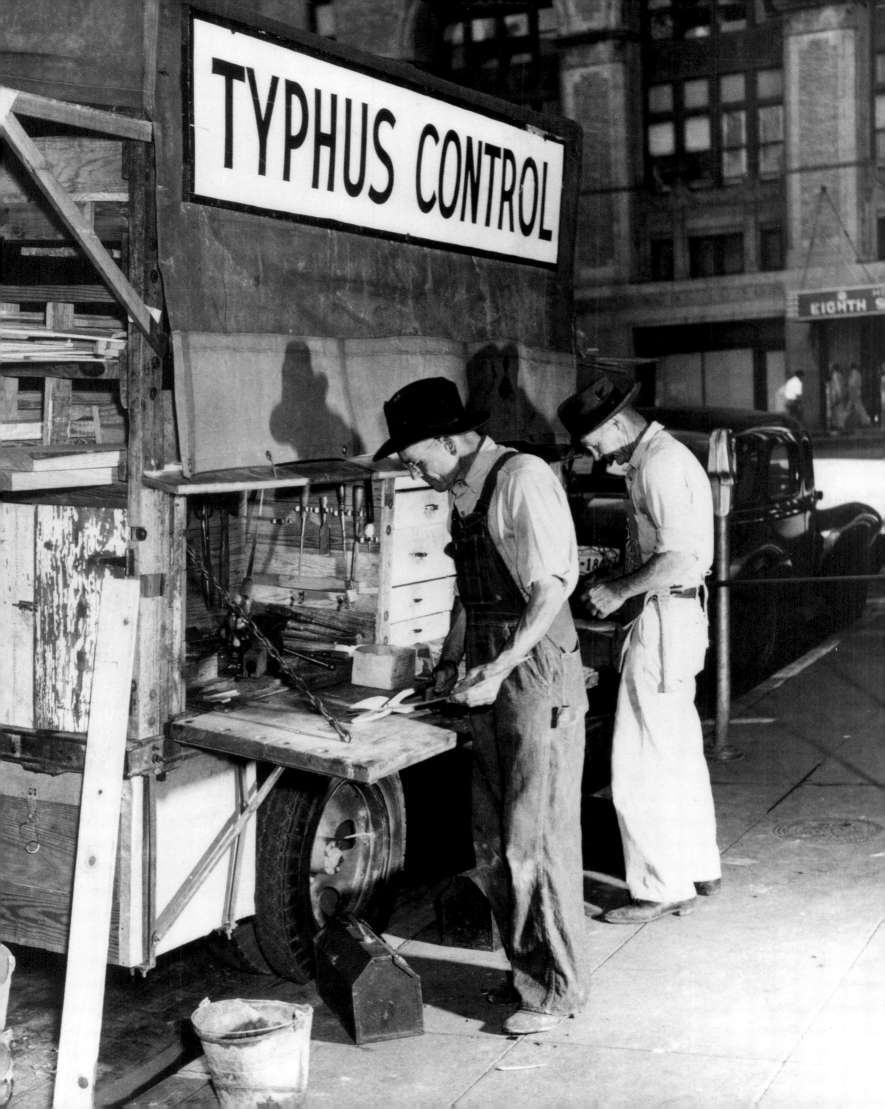

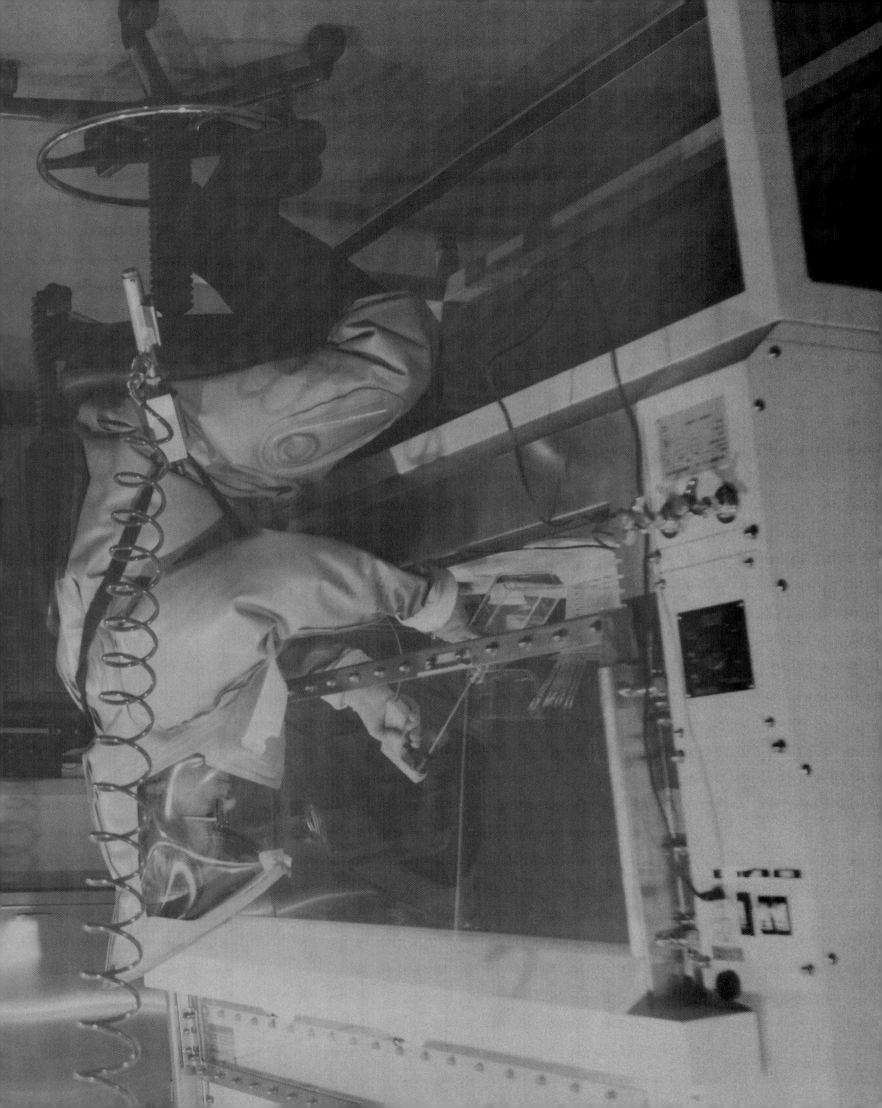

Chapter 6

... $\mathcal{M}$any common disease-causing **bacteria** are becoming **resistant to** antibiotic treatment, raising **Serious implications**...

Diseases Conquered,
Deadly Successors

1 9 4 9   t o   p r e s e n t

With the end of World War II, **US medical researchers** turned their attention to what were hoped to be the final frontiers of infectious disease control and treatment. At the top of their priority list was poliomyelitis. By the late 1940s, polio had become the most feared "plague" in the public's mind. Unlike many earlier contagious diseases, polio seemed to have a particular affinity for the middle and upper classes whose living conditions were generally sanitary and uncrowded, so efforts to avert its spread through neighborhood cleanups and quarantines were judged irrelevant. As the disease most often struck during the warm months, prudent parents kept vacationing children at home, away from movie theaters, public swimming pools, and playgrounds where the mysterious virus was thought to lurk. Still, the numbers of infected rose, from 10 000 in 1940, to 25 000 in 1946, to 57 000 in 1953. Children continued to be the chief targets of the disease, though the incidence of polio among soldiers returning from Europe was also considerable.

While the medical community worked on finding better ways to aid and rehabilitate paralyzed victims, public and private funds poured into the search for a polio vaccine. In 1954, Dr. Jonas Salk, with support from the National Foundation for

Infantile Paralysis, announced that he had developed a killed-virus serum capable of immunizing humans against any one of three strains of the polio virus. A year later, fol-

lowing extensive field trials, the Food and Drug Administration endorsed Salk's vaccine, launching a nationwide drive to get every child in the country inoculated. In 1957, Salk's colleague, Dr. Albert Sabin, brought forth his own polio vaccine containing a live but weakened strain of the virus.

> Pharmaceutical science has also continued to develop new drugs and medications to fight the world's diseases, using revolutionary new techniques to create substances that more precisely match disease processes with chemicals to inhibit them.

Administered orally, the Sabin vaccine ultimately became the preferred method of protection. Within a very few years, the public's fear of polio virtually disappeared. Smallpox, another once-terrifying disease, also lost its sting, and was declared officially extinct by the World Health Organization in 1977.

Pharmaceutical science has also continued to develop new drugs and medications to fight the world's diseases, using revolutionary new techniques to create substances that more precisely match disease processes with chemicals to inhibit them. Today's armamentarium of disease-fighting drugs includes not only scores of classic antibiotics, but synthetic antibiotics known as antibacterials, including the highly effective group known as quinolones. Antivirals, antiprotozoals, anthelmintics, and antifungals—some broad spectrum and some of singular application—are also among the offerings.

But if the control of these and many other more ancient plagues and pestilences can be counted as remarkable success stories today, the public and the medical community have had plenty of other reasons to remain vigilant. New diseases of fearsome dimension have continued to surface and almost certainly will do so in the future. The World Health Organization estimates that in 1997 nearly 50 000 people around the globe died each day as the direct result of an infectious disease.

Perhaps the best known of the apparently new crop of infectious diseases is AIDS, the common name for acquired immunodeficiency syndrome. Official recognition of this deadly disease was declared in June 1981, when the Centers for Disease Control included in its weekly morbidity report the existence of five cases of a rare form of pneumonia among a group of Los Angeles homosexuals. In the next few months, the Centers for

Disease Control would report other clusters of virulent opportunistic infections among intravenous drug users, female prostitutes, heterosexual Haitians and Africans, and still later among hemophiliacs and

> The World Health Organization estimates that in 1997 nearly 50 000 people around the globe died each day as the direct result of an infectious disease.

infants born to AIDS-infected mothers. With the number of known cases doubling every six months, and with persons of every race, age, and social group eventually being drawn into the statistical picture, researchers in a number of countries mobilized to identify the cause and find ways to prevent the disease's spread. In 1984, the causative HIV virus was isolated and a diagnostic test developed to identify human carriers. At a relatively early stage in the research, it was also deduced that AIDS probably originated in nonhuman primates, perhaps among monkeys living in the rain forests of Africa. Medical detectives concluded that the HIV virus most likely escaped into the human population through simple contact, a reminder that infectious organisms dwelling more or less without con-sequence in animal hosts can hold the potential to mutate and become the prime source of human contagion.

Since 1990, several drugs capable of slowing the replication of HIV virus and its secondary infections have given hope to millions. Several AIDS vaccines are also being tested, offering some promise of protection in the future to persons at risk. At the same time, many common disease-causing bacteria are becoming resistant to antibiotic treatment, raising serious implications for the control of some bacterial diseases in the years to come. *Staphylococcus aureus*, one of the most deadly species of bacteria and a prime cause of hospital infections, is a vivid case in point: a mutant strain resistant to antibiotics has lately been reported in a Japanese hospital. Health experts say it is only a matter of time before it arrives in the United States.

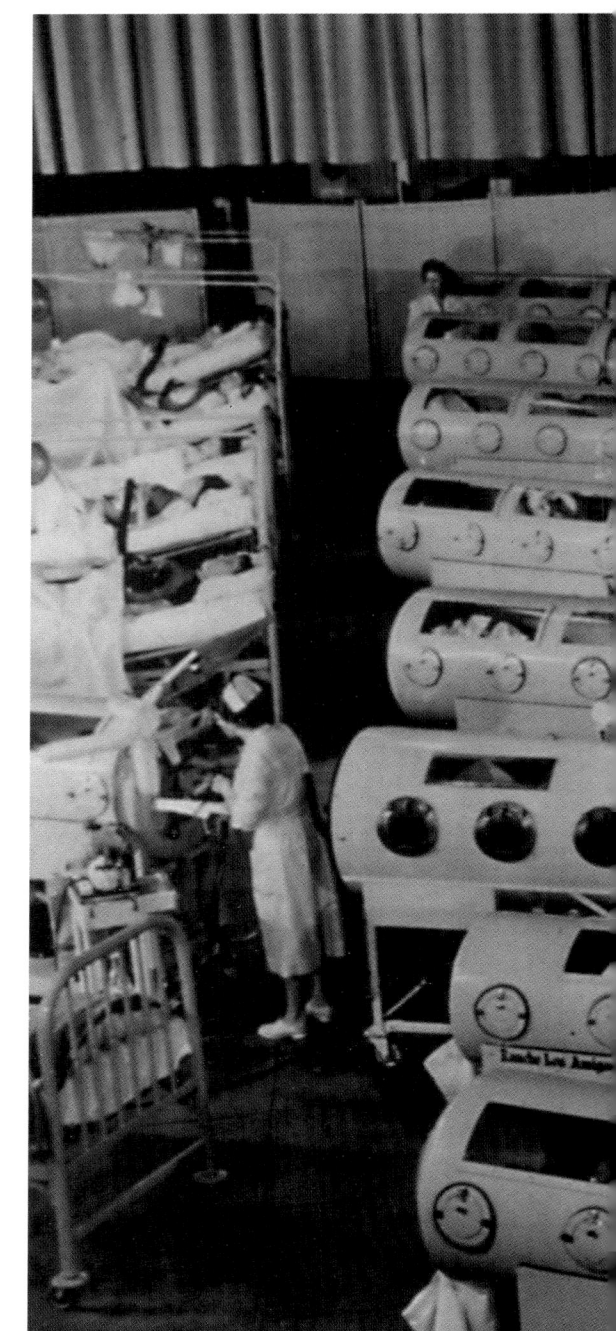

World health experts warn, too, that several extra-ordinarily lethal viruses—the fast-acting Ebola, Lassa, Marburg, and Hanta, and several slow viruses, to name just the most notorious of the newly identified pathogens—are emerging in scattered parts of the world. Any and all of them, say the scientists, are capable of triggering deadly epidemics if we, as an international community, fail to be prudent in the way we live our lives and the manner in which we manipulate our environments.

THE AVERAGE AMERICAN INFANT in the years immediately following World War II was immunized against whooping cough, tetanus, diphtheria, smallpox, and tuberculosis—all classic killers in centuries past. But poliomyelitis was still a threat to the populace and children in particular. Indeed, the numbers of infected continued to rise. In 1952, the worst year on record, close to 58 000 cases were reported. As many fell victim to bulbar polio and paralysis, they could only survive the acute phase with the support of mechanical respirators, like the cumbersome "iron lungs" shown at Rancho Los Amigos Medical Center, Downey, California.

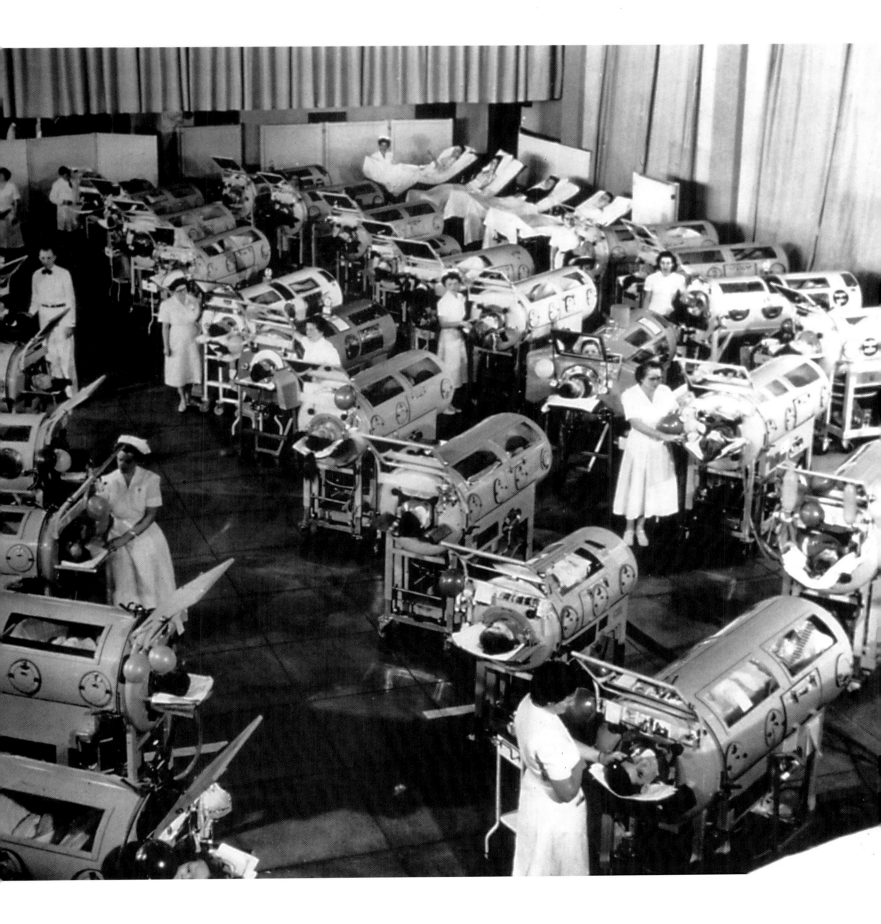

BETWEEN 1951 AND 1953, GAMMA GLOBULIN was tested as a preventive, but after extensive field trials it was found that the immunity was short-lived and consequently abandoned. The following year, Dr. Jonas Salk, working at the Virus Research Laboratory at the University of Pittsburgh, introduced an inoculant made of killed polio virus. More than 1 830 000 school-children were involved in a rigorous double-blind test that year. Marched into gymnasiums at selected schools all over the country, each child was given a shot and a large button proclaiming the wearer as a "Polio Pioneer."

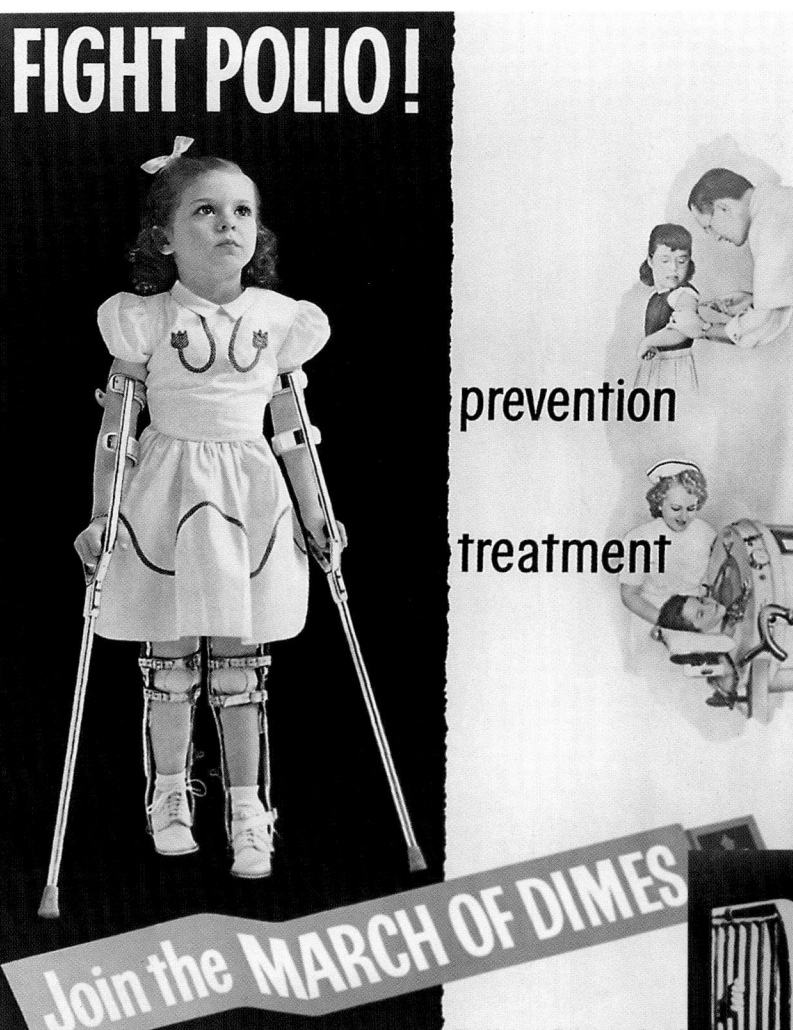

FIGHT POLIO !

prevention

treatment

Join the **MARCH OF DIMES**

The National Foundation for Infa...

TO RAISE FUNDS FOR RESEARCH and for the care of so many sick and crippled children, the National Foundation for Infantile Paralysis continually looked for ways to gain broader financial support. As momentum gathered, annual costs to the Foundation hovered in the $20-million range, most of it provided by individual donors. One particularly effective device was the annual polio poster, which was introduced in 1946 and was displayed in public places around the country. Each year an appealing poster child was selected to represent the fund drive. Shown are young Donald Anderson (right), who appeared on the 1946 poster, and Mary Kosloski (above), featured in 1955.

Your dimes did this for me!

JOIN the MARCH of DIMES
JANUARY 14-31

THE NATIONAL FOUNDATION FOR INFANTILE PARALYSIS, INC
FRANKLIN D. ROOSEVELT, FOUNDER

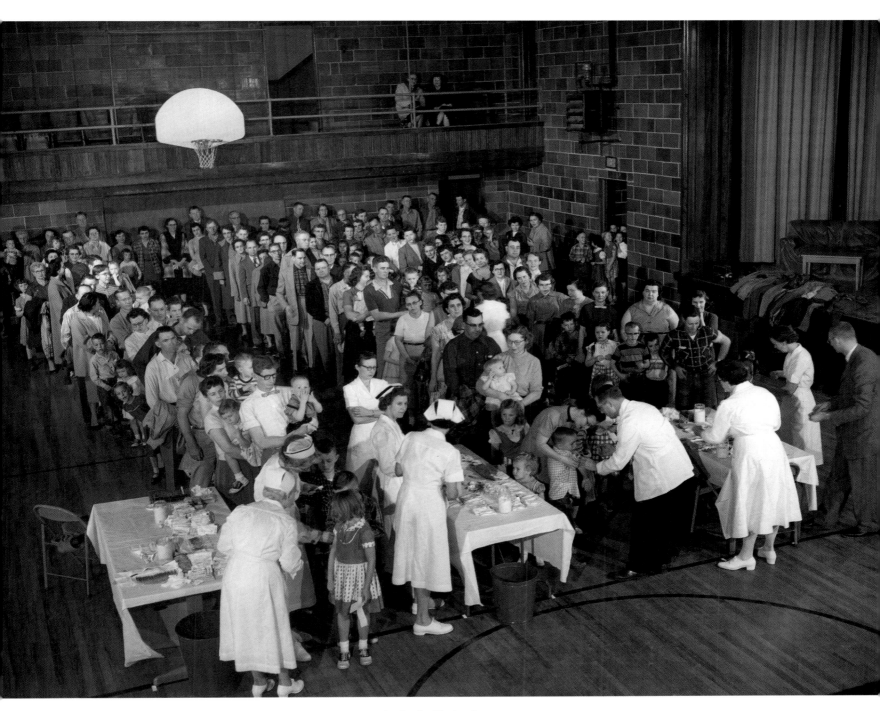

ON THE TENTH ANNIVERSARY OF FRANKLIN ROOSEVELT'S death, the National Foundation announced that independent examiners had determined the Salk vaccine to be both safe and effective in conferring permanent immunity. Immediately, the FDA gave six pharmaceutical companies the green light to produce the vaccine commercially. Before summer 1955 had ended, 4 000 000 doses had been administered in a nationwide campaign. Scenes like the one above in Protection, Kansas, were commonplace.

DR. JONAS SALK became an overnight national hero. Here, he is seen examining batches of his polio vaccine. Remarkable as his achievement was, his colleague and rival, Dr. Albert Sabin, eventually produced an even better form of protection in his attenuated live-virus vaccine. Introduced in 1964, the Sabin vaccine has since become the treatment of choice.

ANOTHER DISEASE TO COME UNDER CONTROL in the 1960s was rubella, or German measles. Two NIH researchers, Dr. Harry M. Meyer, Jr., shown left, and Dr. Paul D. Parkman, right, developed the live-virus vaccine in 1965 while working at the Division of Biologics Standards. Rubella vaccine became available to the public two years later.

AS MANY OF THE MOST DANGEROUS contagions
were contained, researchers began looking
into other, less hazardous infections.
Sneezing, which had long been recognized
as a mode of transmission for the common
cold and possibly other infections, became
a mechanism worth studying. One mode of
study was with high-speed photography, as
demonstrated by Harold Edgerton's famous
1/30 000-second exposure for MIT researcher
Marshall W. Jennison. By analyzing photos
like this one, Jennison determined that a
single sneeze can contain over 4500 droplets
of virus-laden mucus and that such infectious materials can be propelled up to 12
feet away at speeds of more than 100 mph.

THE US PUBLIC HEALTH SERVICE remains active
in other forms of international disease
control. Dr. Hildrus Poindexter, experienced
in tropical diseases, is one such medical
missionary for the Public Health Service.
Beginning in the years after World War II,
Poindexter was posted to Liberia, Suriname,
Iraq, Libya, Jamaica, and Sierra Leone.

SMALLPOX WAS BROUGHT under effective control in the United States by 1962. When the World Health Organization decided in 1967 to attempt the disease's eradication on a global scale, it called upon the expertise of the Centers for Disease Control. Specialists in infectious disease were sent out to train national medical teams at many locations. Here, a local technician uses a high-speed jet injector to administer a shot in the arm of a West African tribesman. So successful did the program prove that the last case of smallpox was recorded in 1977. Three years later, World Health Organization officials declared the disease eradicated.

ACQUIRED IMMUNODEFICIENCY SYNDROME entered the public consciousness in the 1980s. The first evidence of the new disease was recorded in 1981, when a number of homosexuals fell ill and died with alarming speed. By the end of 1982, nearly 1600 cases had been reported worldwide, and the infected represented an increasingly broad spectrum of the population. Initially, the cause of the disease was difficult to detect, because much of what appeared to be AIDS—Kaposi's sarcoma, pneumonia, and other conditions—were actually the secondary results of the infection. Not until 1984 did researchers at laboratories in Paris and Bethesda, Maryland, simultaneously isolate the fundamental agent of AIDS, a retrovirus that attacks the immune system, leaving the body vulnerable to a range of exotic diseases. Leading the American team was Dr. Robert Gallo at the National Cancer Institute, shown above. As the so-called HIV virus produces a tell-tale antibody in the blood of infected persons, it became possible as early as 1985 to test for infection and to screen the public blood supply for presence of the disease. Government campaigns, including the poster (right), were initiated to educate the public.

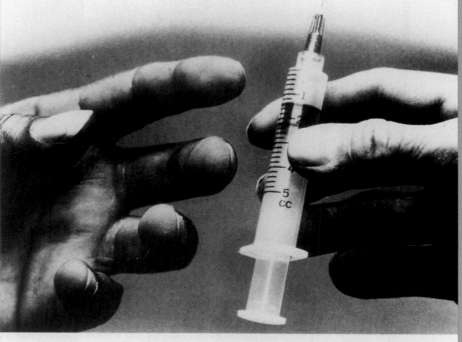

SHARING NEEDLES CAN GET YOU MORE THAN HIGH.

IT CAN GET YOU AIDS.

You can't tell if someone has the AIDS virus just by looking.

You can't tell if needles or works are infected just by looking.

When you shoot drugs and share needles or works you could get AIDS. Even if you think your drug-sharing partners are clean, if the AIDS virus is present, it could be passed to you.

AIDS is not pretty. It's a long, slow, painful way to die. Do the right thing. Get into treatment. It's the best way to make sure you don't shoot up AIDS.

STOP SHOOTING UP AIDS.
GET INTO DRUG TREATMENT
CALL 1-800 662 HELP.

TO DRAMATIZE THE ENORMOUS LOSS OF LIFE due to the disease, a group calling themselves the Names Project Foundation was formed in 1986. Inviting friends and family of the deceased to prepare commemorative sections of decorative embroidery and patchwork for a vast Memorial Quilt, the sponsoring group was overwhelmed by submissions in no time. On the tenth anniversary of the project, Names organizers laid their work before Congress, literally, as part of the effort to increase funding for AIDS research. They spread the quilt on the mall at the foot of the Washington Monument. By this time, the quilt had grown to nearly 43 000 sections, enough to fill 16 football fields.

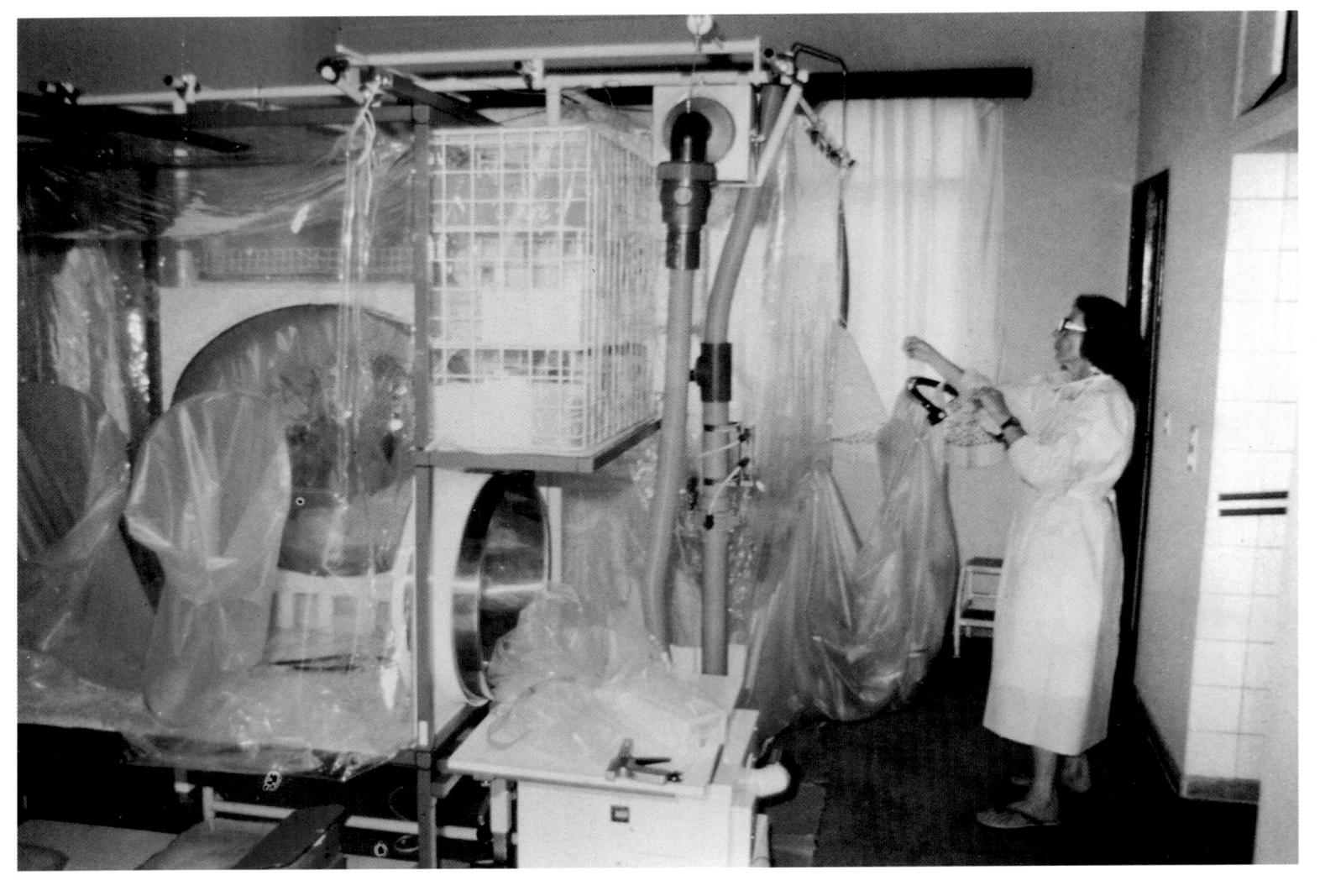

AS THE WORLD BECOMES SMALLER and travel to the most distant communities ever more commonplace, the spread of diseases for which huge numbers of the population are entirely vulnerable becomes an ever more pressing concern to epidemiologists and public health officials. One of the first of the dangerous new breed of epidemic diseases is a form of hemorrhagic fever that first appeared in Marburg, Germany, in 1967 among a group of laboratory workers. The lab technicians were working with imported African green monkeys, and it was eventually discovered that a strain of monkey virus had mutated beyond its usual animal host range to enter the human population. To contain the disease, patients were isolated in plastic tents, like the ones shown above, and medical personnel were required to tend them according to the most stringent sanitary protocols.

DANGEROUS AS THE NEWER EMERGING DISEASES are now recognized to be, scientists working in the field have not always been cautious in their methodology. Here, the Centers for Disease Control's Dr. Vern Newhouse studies a lineup of rodents while investigating Lassa fever in Sierra Leone in 1972, three years after it was first reported in West Africa. It is now known that the virus is harbored by a type of rat and that infection may be acquired by inhaling droplets of the rat's urine or through contact with the blood or sputum of an infected person.

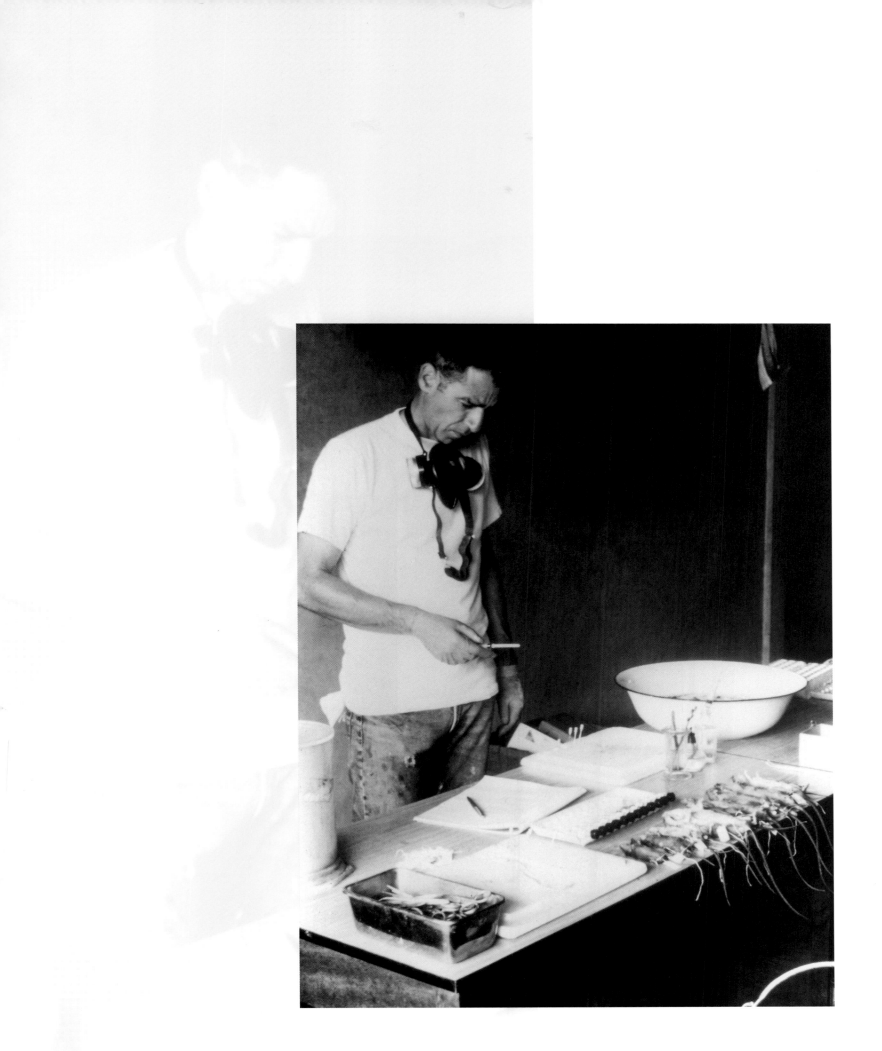

BIO-CONTAINMENT IS NOW THE STANDARD for much of infectious disease research and for the research that ultimately produces new drugs and new vaccines. Shown above, two women in full-body protective suits and helmets run routine tests on benches shielded under glass hoods. Air circulation is closely controlled by a battery of ventilators that constantly neutralize dangerous airborne organisms.

AT THE MAXIMUM CONTAINMENT LABORATORY at the Centers for Disease Control in Atlanta, Georgia, technicians carry out a "specimen transfer" through gloved ports. The setup allows two fully protected researchers to pass materials under conditions of total isolation.

Bibliography

BETTMANN OC. *A Pictorial History of Medicine*. New York, NY: Charles C. Thomas; 1956.

BOLLET AJ. *Plagues & Poxes*. New York, NY: Demos Publications; 1987.

COLLIER R. *The Plague of the Spanish Lady*: *The Influenza Pandemic of 1918-1919*. New York, NY: Atheneum; 1974.

DONAHUE PM. *Nursing, the Finest Art*. St. Louis, Mo: CV Mosby; 1985.

DUFFY J. *The Healers, A History of American Medicine*. Urbana, Ill: University of Chicago Press; 1976.

GALLAGHER R. *Diseases That Plague Modern Man*; *A History of Ten Communicable Diseases*. Dobbs Ferry, NY: Oceana Publications; 1969.

GARRETT L. *The Coming Plague: Newly Emerging Diseases in a World Out of Balance*. New York, NY: Harper Collins; 1994.

GARRISON FH. *An Introduction to the History of Medicine*. Philadelphia, Pa: WB Saunders Co; 1929.

GOLDIN G. *Work of Mercy: A Pictorial History of Hospitals*. Ontario, Canada: The Boston Mills Press; 1994.

HAGGARD HW. *Devils, Drugs, and Doctors*. New York, NY: Harper & Brothers; 1929.

KIPLE KF. *Cambridge World History of Human Disease*. Cambridge, UK: Cambridge University Press; 1993.

KOHN GC. *Encyclopedia of Plague and Pestilence*. New York, NY: Facts on File; 1995.

LYONS AS, PETRUCELLI RJ. *Medicine, An Illustrated History*. New York, NY: Abradale Press & Harry N. Abrams; 1987.

MCCULLOUGH D. *The Path Between the Seas*. New York, NY: Simon & Schuster; 1977.

MCGREW RE. *Encyclopedia of Medical History*. New York, NY: McGraw-Hill Book Co; 1985.

MCNEIL WH. *Plagues and Peoples*. New York, NY: Doubleday; 1976.

MULLEN F. *Plagues and Politics, The Story of the US Public Health Service*. New York, NY: Basic Books; 1989.

NAYTHONS M. *The Face of Mercy: A Photographic History of Medicine at War*. New York, NY: Random House; 1993.

NOVOTNY A, SMITH C. *Images of Healing*. New York, NY: Macmillan; 1980.

OTT K. *Fevered Lives, Tuberculosis in American Culture Since 1870*. Cambridge, Mass: Harvard University Press; 1996.

RHODES R. *Deadly Feasts, Tracking the Secrets of a Terrifying New Plague*. New York, NY: Simon & Schuster; 1997.

SMITH JS. *Patenting the Sun, Polio and the Salk Vaccine*. New York, NY: Anchor Doubleday; 1990.

VIOLA HJ, MARGOLIS C. *Seeds of Change, Five Hundred Years Since Columbus*. Washington, DC: Smithsonian Institution Press; 1991.

WILLS C. *Yellow Fever, Black Goddess*. New York, NY: Harper Collins; 1996.

WOOD WB. *From Miasmas to Molecules*. New York, NY: Columbia University Press; 1961.

Photo Credits

Grateful acknowledgement is made to the following for providing photographs for this book:

BAKKEN LIBRARY AND MUSEUM,
Minneapolis, Minnesota–72, 73

CENTERS FOR DISEASE CONTROL AND PREVENTION,
Atlanta, Georgia–145, 148, 149, 150, 151

ALAN MASON CHESNEY MEDICAL ARCHIVES OF
THE JOHNS HOPKINS MEDICAL INSTITUTIONS,
Baltimore, Maryland–64, 65

CHICAGO HISTORICAL SOCIETY,
Chicago, Illinois–103 (top)

CHILDREN'S HOSPITAL,
Boston, Massachusetts–78-79 (background),
103 (bottom)

COLLECTION OF THE CORCORAN GALLERY OF ART,
Washington, DC, Gift of Mrs. Alice Fries King, in
memory of her father–70

CORBIS-BETTMANN, New York, New York–15, 16,
19, 21, 22

DIVISION OF MEDICAL SCIENCES, SMITHSONIAN
MUSEUMS, NATIONAL MUSEUM OF AMERICAN
HISTORY, Washington, DC–26, 49, 53, 63 (bottom),
71 (top left)

THE HAROLD E. EDGERTON 1992 TRUST, Courtesy
of The Palm Press, Inc, Concord, Massachusetts–140
(background), 141

IOWA STATE UNIVERSITY LIBRARY/UNIVERSITY
ARCHIVES, Ames, Iowa–2-3, 108-109

LIBRARY OF CONGRESS, Washington, DC–40, 54,
58, 59 (top), 67, 68, 69, 76 (top left), 79, 105,
128 (left), 129

MARCH OF DIMES, White Plains, New York–111
(right), 122, 123, 134-135, 136-137, 138, 139,
140 (top)

MASSACHUSETTS HISTORICAL SOCIETY, Boston,
Massachusetts–23

MENCZER MUSEUM OF MEDICINE AND DENTISTRY,
Hartford, Connecticut–71 (top and bottom left)

MINNESOTA HISTORICAL SOCIETY, St. Paul,
Minnesota–90, 110-111, 115

MUSEUM OF THE CITY OF NEW YORK, New York–44

MUSEUM OF THE CITY OF NEW YORK, Brown
Brothers, New York, New York–7, 66

MUSEUM OF THE CITY OF NEW YORK, Byron
Collection, New York, New York–91

MÜTTER MUSEUM, Philadelphia College of Physicians,
Philadelphia, Pennsylvania–14-15, 25, 27

THE NAMES PROJECT FOUNDATION,
San Francisco, California–146-147

NATIONAL ARCHIVES, Washington, DC–54 (left),
56-57, 68, 71 (bottom), 93, 94, 100, 101,
106-107, 116-117, 118, 120 (top), 121

NATIONAL CANCER INSTITUTE & US PUBLIC HEALTH
SERVICE, Bethesda, Maryland–144

NATIONAL LIBRARY OF MEDICINE, Bethesda,
Maryland–14, 20, 29 (top), 35, 36, 37, 38, 39 (background), 41, 44 (background), 45, 46, 47, 48, 49
(background), 60, 62-63, 63, 76 (background), 77,
82, 83, 84, 85, 86, 87 (left and background), 95,
96 (left), 104, 109, 119, 120 (bottom), 125,
127 (right)

NEW YORK ACADEMY OF MEDICINE LIBRARY,
New York, New York–28

NORMAN PUBLISHING, San Francisco, California,
Facsimile reprint edition of George Tiemann & Co,
American Armamentarium Chirurgicum, and Menczer
Museum of Medicine and Dentistry, Hartford,
Connecticut–59 (bottom), 71 (right)

NORWALK HOSPITAL, Norwalk, Connecticut.
Photographer: Debranne Cingari–39

PHILADELPHIA MUSEUM OF ART, Philadelphia,
Pennsylvania, Gift of Mrs. William H.
Horstmann–11, 30-31, 32, 42-43

PROGRAM SUPPORT CENTER, DEPARTMENT OF
HEALTH AND HUMAN SERVICES, Rockville,
Maryland–13, 29 (bottom), 74, 75, 92, 102, 126-127,
128-129, 130-131, 132, 140 (bottom), 142, 143,
150, 156

ROCKEFELLER ARCHIVE CENTER, Sleepy Hollow,
New York–81, 96-97, 98, 99

SARANAC FREE LIBRARY, Adirondack Collection,
Saranac Lake, New York–88, 89

STATE HISTORICAL SOCIETY OF WISCONSIN,
Visual Materials Archive, Madison, Wisconsin–114

TEMPLE UNIVERSITY, Urban Archives, Philadelphia,
Pennsylvania–124, 125 (background)

YALE UNIVERSITY, Harvey Cushing/John Hay
Whitney Medical Library, New Haven, Connecticut–24,
34, 50-51, 54-55, 61